Christology

Knowing Jesus Christ

Gregory Brown

Publishing

Endorsements

"The Bible Teacher's Guide … will help any teacher study and get a better background for his/her Bible lessons. In addition, it will give direction and scope to teaching of the Word of God. Praise God for this contemporary introduction to the Word of God."

—Dr. Elmer Towns
Co-founder of Liberty University
Former Dean, Liberty Baptist Theological Seminary

"Expositional, theological, and candidly practical! I highly recommend The Bible Teacher's Guide for anyone seeking to better understand or teach God's Word."

—Dr. Young–Gil Kim
Founding President, Handong Global University

"Helpful to both the layman and the serious student, The Bible Teacher's Guide, by Dr. Greg Brown, is outstanding!"

—Dr. Neal Weaver
President, Louisiana Baptist University

"Whether you are preparing a Bible study, a sermon, or simply wanting to dive deeper into a personal study of God's Word, these will be very helpful tools."

—Eddie Byun
Associate Professor of Christian Ministry, Biola University
Author of Justice Awakening

"I am happy that Greg is making his insights into God's truth available to a wider audience through these books. They bear the hallmarks of good Bible teaching: the result of rigorous Bible study and thoroughgoing application to the lives of people."

—Ajith Fernando
Teaching Director, Youth for Christ
Author of A Call to Joy and Pain

"The content of the series is rich. My prayer is that God will use it to help the body of Christ grow strong."

—Dr. Min Chung
Senior Pastor, Covenant Fellowship Church, Urbana, Illinois
Adjunct Professor, Urbana Theological Seminary

"Knowing the right questions to ask and how to go about answering them is fundamental to learning in any subject matter. Greg demonstrates this convincingly."

—Dr. William Moulder

Professor of Biblical Studies, Trinity International University

"Pastor Greg is passionate about the Word of God, rigorous and thorough in his approach to the study of it... I am pleased to recommend The Bible Teacher's Guide to anyone who hungers for the living Word."

—Dr. JunMo Cho
Professor of Linguistics, Handong Global University
Contemporary Christian Music Recording Artist

"I can't imagine any student of Scripture not benefiting by this work."

—Steven J. Cole
Pastor, Flagstaff Christian Fellowship, Flagstaff, Arizona
Author of the Riches from the Word series

"Greg deals with the principles, doctrines, and applications of the text in a practical way which is useful for both individual growth or for help in preparation for teaching."

—Bob Deffinbaugh
Ministry Coordinator, Bible.org
Founding Pastor, Community Bible Chapel, Richardson, Texas

Content

Preface

And entrust what you heard me say in the presence of many others as witnesses to faithful people who will be competent to teach others as well.
2 Timothy 2:2 (NET)

Paul's words to Timothy still apply to us today. The church needs teachers who clearly and fearlessly teach the Word of God. With this in mind, The Bible Teacher's Guide (BTG) series was created. This series includes both expositional and topical studies, with resources to help teachers lead small groups, pastors prepare sermons, and individuals increase their knowledge of God's Word.

Christology can be used for personal study or as a nine-session small group curriculum, depending on how the leader divides up the topics. For small groups, the members will read a chapter (or chapters) and discuss the reflection questions and anything else that stood out in the reading within their gathering. Or, the chapter can be read before the gathering, with the meeting focusing only on discussion.

Introduction

Now this is eternal life—that they know you, the only true God, and Jesus Christ, whom you sent.
John 17:3

Who is Jesus Christ? This question elicits a lot of mystery and confusion. Some say Jesus was only a regular human—maybe a wise man or prophet. Others say he is a created being, like an angel. Still, others say Jesus is God but not human. While others say he is both fully God and fully human. Who exactly is Jesus? Scripture teaches that our eternal destiny depends on how we answer this question (1 John 4:2-3, Rom 10:9-10); therefore, it befits us to reflect on this question and answer it correctly. In this study, we'll consider what the Bible says about Jesus Christ, so that we may enjoy the eternal life, which only comes through him (John 3:16, 17:3) and also know, worship, and serve him in a more excellent manner (Rev 5:11-14). May God the Father, Christ the Son, and the Holy Spirit richly bless your study!

Christ's Preexistence and Deity

Scripture does not teach that Christ came into existence at his birth or that he was a created being, as some errantly teach. He always existed. Many Scriptures teach this: Micah 5:2 says, "As for you, Bethlehem Ephrathah, seemingly insignificant among the clans of Judah— from you a king will emerge who will rule over Israel on my behalf, one whose origins are in the distant past." Micah predicted that the messiah would be born in Bethlehem and that he would be the future king of Israel. However, Micah says that he had existed from "the distant past" or "ancient times" (NIV). Isaiah 9:6 says, "For a child has been born to us, a son has been given to us. He shoulders responsibility and is called: Extraordinary Strategist, Mighty God, Everlasting Father, Prince of Peace." Isaiah predicted that a child would be born who would be called "Everlasting Father," which means that this person, though born in time, had existed forever. In fact, Jesus said something similar about himself in John 8:58, which caused him to be mocked. He said, "… I tell you the solemn truth, before Abraham came into existence, I am!" When Christ said this, it was not just a reference to his preexistence, but also his deity. When God introduced himself to Israel during their slavery in Egypt, he introduced himself by the name "I Am" (Ex 3:14) and so did Christ. Christ has always existed, since he is God.

Christ's Deity

As mentioned, not only has Christ always existed, he has eternally existed as God. This is the central aspect of Christ's person, which many have questioned, struggled with, and denied. Certainly, his deity and eternality are hard to fathom. Yet, this is exactly what Scripture teaches. The author of Hebrews gives God the Father's testimony about his Son in Hebrews 1:8, saying, "Your throne, O God, is forever and ever, and a righteous scepter is the scepter of your kingdom." In the context, the author of Hebrews argues for the greatness of Christ by comparing him to angels. He does this by quoting God's words about the Son in Psalm 45:6. God the Father calls the Son, "God," which God never said about an angel.

In addition, John 1:1-3 says,

> In the beginning was the Word, and the Word was with God, and the Word was fully God. The Word was with God in the beginning. All things were created by him, and apart from him not one thing was created that has been created.

John gives Jesus the title, "the Word," which means that Christ is the communication of God—the way we get to know more about God and his will. Then John says that "the Word" was "with God," "was fully God," and also that the Word created all things. This is a clear declaration of Christ's deity.

Paul makes the same declaration about Christ in Colossians 1:15-16:

> He is the image of the invisible God, the firstborn over all creation, for all things in heaven and on earth were created by him—all things, whether visible or invisible, whether thrones or dominions, whether principalities or powers—all things were created through him and for him.

Jesus is the visible image of the invisible God, and he is the Creator of the earth. When God the Father created the earth, he did it through the Son and for the Son (Col 1:16).

Likewise, Peter said this about Jesus in 2 Peter 1:1, "From Simeon Peter, a slave and apostle of Jesus Christ, to those who through the righteousness of our God and Savior, Jesus Christ, have been granted a faith just as precious as ours." Peter didn't just call Jesus, "Savior," but also "God."

Further evidence for Christ's deity is the fact that Jesus' contemporaries commonly called him "Lord." When they did this, they were employing a term (Kurios) that was used over 6,814 times in the Septuagint, the Greek translation of the Old Testament, to refer to God.[1] Wayne Grudem said this about the use of the term:

> Therefore, any Greek-speaking reader at the time of the New Testament who had any knowledge at all of the Greek Old Testament would have recognized that, in contexts where it was appropriate, the word "Lord" was the name of the one who was the Creator and Sustainer of heaven and earth, the omnipotent God.[2]

Consequently, when the angels announced Jesus' birth by saying, "Today your Savior is born in the city of David. He is Christ the Lord." (Luke 2:11), they were saying that Jesus was the Lord God.

Finally, evidence for Christ's deity is the fact that he accepted worship. In John 5:23, Christ said: "The one who does not honor the Son does not honor the Father who sent him." Essentially, that means if we don't worship Jesus, we can't worship God. Also, in John 9, after healing a blind man, Christ asked him if he believed in the Son of man (v. 35). After Christ revealed himself as the messiah, the man responded with, "'Lord, I believe,' and he worshiped him" (v. 38). In addition, after revealing himself to Thomas after his resurrection, Thomas said to Christ, "My Lord and my God!" (John 20:28). The blind man's and Thomas' responses are especially amazing considering they were monotheistic Jews, who believed that only God deserved worship and worshipping anything or anyone else brought God's judgment (Ex 20:4-6). Daryl Aaron said this about their worship of Jesus:

> In historical context, what they did was absolutely revolutionary. And Jesus did not rebuke them. If thinking that he was God had revealed a terrible misunderstanding, Jesus could have taken the opportunity to say, "Hold on! Don't worship me! Worship only God" (as, for instance, Paul and Barnabas did, and as angels repeatedly did). Jesus accepted worship because he is God and is worthy of it.[3]

Distinct

With all that said, though Scripture teaches Christ's preexistence and deity, it also teaches that Jesus is "distinct" or separate from God. When talking to unbelieving Jews, Christ said this about himself in John 10:35-36:

> If those people to whom the word of God came were called 'gods' (and the scripture cannot be broken), do you say about the one whom the Father set apart and sent into the world, 'You are blaspheming,' because I said, 'I am the Son of God'?

In calling himself "Son of God," Christ was not only emphasizing his equality with God but declaring that he was distinct from God.

We get a great picture of this distinctness at his baptism. Matthew 3:16-17 says:

17

After Jesus was baptized, just as he was coming up out of the water, the heavens opened and he saw the Spirit of God descending like a dove and coming on him. And a voice from heaven said, "This is my one dear Son; in him I take great delight."

Clearly, in this passage, God the Father is separate from the Son, as God declares his pleasure in the Son. Also, the Holy Spirit is distinct as he falls on the Son.

Unity

In addition, Scripture also teaches Christ's unity with God. In John 10:30, Christ said, "The Father and I are one." Also, in John 10:38, he said, "…I am in the Father and the Father is in me."

Jesus is God, and yet distinct from God, and at the same time unified with him. This is the doctrine of the Trinity, as the Holy Spirit is also distinctly God and yet unified with them. It is a mystery, which does not make perfect sense to us, but it is repeatedly taught in Scripture.

Daryl Aaron's comments on the importance of Christ's deity for the church historically are a helpful conclusion to this section of our study:

It is no surprise that from very early on, believers have contended for, fought for, and died for this teaching—the deity of Jesus Christ. In a nutshell, the doctrine is that Jesus Christ is fully God (not half God or one-third God) and eternally God (he did not become God at some point in time). Anything less has been considered heresy.[4]

One of the reasons this doctrine is so crucial is that if Jesus is not fully God, there is no salvation to be found in his death. The sacrifice that would be sufficient for the many sins of the many people had to be a sacrifice of infinite value. No human being could provide this kind of sacrifice; only God himself could. This is why the early Christians were so appalled at the deity of Jesus being denied. They knew his deity was absolutely vital for their salvation.[5]

Application

How should we apply Christ's preexistence and deity? Since Jesus is eternally God (Is 9:6), we should worship and pray to him, even as we do the other members of the Godhead. In John 14:14, Christ taught his disciples to pray to him when he said, "If you ask me anything in my name, I will do it." Likewise, in Revelation 22:17, the Spirit and the church pray to Christ, asking him to return, and others are encouraged to pray the same way. "And the Spirit and the bride say, 'Come!' And let the one who hears say: 'Come!'" Finally, in Revelation 5:11-14, all the inhabitants of heaven and earth worship Christ for his great sacrifice:

> Then I looked and heard the voice of many angels in a circle around the throne, as well as the living creatures and the elders. Their number was ten thousand times ten thousand—thousands times thousands—all of whom were singing in a loud voice: "Worthy is the lamb who was killed to receive power and wealth and wisdom and might and honor and glory and praise!" Then I heard every creature— in heaven, on earth, under the earth, in the sea, and all that is in them—singing: "To the one seated on the throne and to the Lamb be praise, honor, glory, and ruling power forever and ever!" And the four living creatures were saying "Amen," and the elders threw themselves to the ground and worshiped.

Since Christ died for us, delivering us from sin and death and giving us his righteousness so we can dwell and rule with him, we should worship and serve him eternally—for he is worthy of all honor, glory, and power! Thank you, Lord!

Reflection

1. What stood out most in the reading and why?
2. What are some common misconceptions about Christ's origin?
3. What are some support verses for the pre-existence of Christ before his birth?
4. What are some support verses for Christ's deity?
5. If somebody asked you to explain the Trinity, how would you explain it?
6. Why should people worship and pray to Jesus? Use Scripture to support.
7. What other questions or applications did you take from the reading?

Christ's Humanity

Scripture not only teaches that Christ eternally pre-existed as God but also that he is human. Isaiah 9:6 says, "For a child has been born to us, a son has been given to us..." The "son" being "given" refers to Christ's deity. He pre-existed as God's eternal Son. However, the phrase "a child is born" refers to the beginning of Christ's humanity, when he was birthed and named Jesus. Before the incarnation, the Son was not a human. Matthew 1:18 speaks of this unique birth: "Now the birth of Jesus Christ happened this way. While his mother Mary was engaged to Joseph, but before they came together, she was found to be pregnant through the Holy Spirit."

In the incarnation, Mary, Jesus' mother, was found with child through the Holy Spirit. The Holy Spirit created a child in her womb without her ever knowing a man sexually. The eternal God became a temporal man; the all-powerful God became a weak baby; the all-knowing God became an infant that grew in knowledge. Luke 2:52 said this about Christ as a child: "And Jesus increased in wisdom and in stature, and in favor with God and with people."

In Christ's humanity, he could be hungry (Matt 4:2), tired, and thirsty (John 4:6-7, 19:28). Like humans, Jesus demonstrated regular emotions, as he wept at Lazarus' grave (John 11:35), felt compassion for people (Matthew 9:36), and even a deep depression before his death. In Matthew 26:38, Christ said, "My soul is overwhelmed with sorrow to the point of death. Stay here and keep watch with me."

This is a mystery we will probably never fully understand until we get to heaven. The merger of Christ's two natures—his deity and humanity—is often called the hypostatic union. Tony Evans defined Christ's hypostatic union as his "undiminished deity and perfect humanity united forever in one person."[6] Incarnation is a related term which refers to Christ becoming human.

The Incarnation

In considering the incarnation, we must ask, "How can Jesus be both fully God and fully human?" A very important text on this is Philippians 2:6-7. It says:

> who though he existed in the form of God did not regard equality with God as something to be grasped, but emptied himself by taking on the form of a slave, by looking like other men, and by sharing in human nature.

Paul here declares that Jesus "existed in the form of God," which simply refers to how Christ preexisted before the incarnation as fully God and equal to God the Father in his deity. Yet, though he was God, he did not consider equality with God something "to be grasped" or held onto. Instead, he "emptied himself," which is the Greek word "kenosis." Christ emptied himself in his incarnation, as he took on human form.

What does it mean for Christ to empty himself in his incarnation? There has been tremendous debate over this throughout history. It can be unequivocally said that Christ did not cease to be God or give up his deity in the incarnation. It is better to think of "emptying himself" as Christ "pouring" his deity into a human body during the incarnation.[7] In this pouring, he limited the attributes of his deity temporarily. The New Living Translation paraphrases "emptied himself" in Philippians 2:7, as "he gave up his divine privileges." For example:

1. In the incarnation, Christ put aside the full use of his divine attributes.

This is seen specifically with the use of his "omniscience." Consider what Jesus told his disciples about his second coming in Matthew 24:36: "But as for that day and hour no one knows it—not even the angels in heaven—except the Father alone." Christ put aside full use of his omniscience while he was on the earth. Some would even argue that Christ never used any of his divine powers while on the earth. He only used the power of God's Spirit, like any faithful follower of God can. We see something of this in his casting out demons. In Matthew 12:28, Christ said, "But if I cast out demons by the Spirit of God, then the kingdom of God has already overtaken you." Christ declared that his casting out demons was not done by his own power but by the Spirit's.

We also see Jesus being filled by the Spirit right after his baptism (Matt 3:16), led into the wilderness by the Spirit (Matt 4:1), and empowered by the Spirit after going through the wilderness temptation. Luke 4:14-15 says this about Christ after he left the wilderness: "Then Jesus, in the power of the Spirit, returned to Galilee, and news about him spread throughout the surrounding countryside. He began to teach in their synagogues and was praised by all." Clearly, the narrator wanted the readers to know that the Holy Spirit was now working through Christ powerfully, as he began his new ministry, which was marked by authoritative preaching and miracles. In the incarnation, Christ temporarily gave up the use of his divine attributes and relied on God's Spirit during his ministry.

2. In the incarnation, Christ put aside his independent freedom as God.

Christ said that he came from heaven not to do his will but the Father's will (John 6:38). In fact, Hebrews 5:8-9 says, "Although he was a son, he learned obedience through the things he suffered. And by being perfected in this way, he became the source of eternal salvation to all who obey him." How did Christ learn obedience in his humanity? Even though Christ has always submitted to the Father (1 Cor. 11:3), as a man, Christ learned obedience to the Father in a way that he never did as God the Son. Isaiah 50:4 gives us insight into this, as it describes the daily routine of our Savior: "The sovereign LORD has given me the capacity to be his spokesman, so that I know how to help the weary. He wakes me up every morning; he makes me alert so I can listen attentively as disciples do." In his humanity, Christ was led like a human; he sought the Lord daily for guidance and empowerment, even as we do. As mentioned, we also see Christ's daily dependence on God in how the Holy Spirit led him after his baptism. Luke 4:1 says, "Then Jesus, full of the Holy Spirit, returned from the Jordan River and was led by the Spirit in the wilderness." In this way, Christ learned obedience. He gave up his independent freedom and was led like a man—the perfect man, who was totally dependent upon the Father.

3. In the incarnation, Christ put aside his glory.

In heaven, he was glorified daily by the angels and the spirits of the righteous men made perfect (Heb 12:22-23); yet, as a man, he took scorn, shame, and being misunderstood. He gave up his glory and put on temporary, frail flesh. In fact, in John 17:5, before going to the cross, Christ prayed that God would restore his previous glory: "And now, Father, glorify me at your side with the glory I had with you before the world was created."

4. In the incarnation, Christ gave up uninterrupted intimacy with God.

At the cross, he was totally separated from God as he cried, "My God, my God, why have you forsaken me?" (Matt 27:46). It seems that at this point on the cross, Christ was bearing the sins of the world and therefore could not have his previous intimacy. He was separated from God, so that we would not have to be eternally separated from God.

Insight on Christological Paradoxes

With all this said, the union of Christ's divine and human natures in the incarnation helps us understand various Christological paradoxes in Scripture. For example, in Christ's humanity, he could be separated from God on the cross (Matt 27:46), but in his deity, he could never be separated. Christ taught that he and the Father were one (John 10:3, 17:21). In Christ's humanity, he was not omnipresent, as he was limited by space and time (John 11:14-15); however, in his deity, he was present everywhere, at all times. In Matthew 18:20, Christ said this to his disciples, "For where two or three are assembled in my name, I am there among them," which reflects an aspect of Christ's omnipresence. In Christ's humanity, he was not omniscient (John 2:24-25). He declared that he didn't even know the time of his coming (Matt 24:36). However, in Christ's deity, he was omniscient, knowing all things. In John 2:24-25, John said this about Christ, "But Jesus would not entrust himself to them, because he knew all people. He did not need anyone to testify about man, for he knew what was in man." Certainly, the union of Christ's divine and human natures in the incarnation is a great mystery that demonstrates the wisdom, power, and glory of God.

The Necessity of the Incarnation

Why was the incarnation necessary? For several reasons:

1. The Son had to become human in order to make atonement for the sins of humans.

An animal's death could not pay for the sins of the world—nor could an angel's death. Christ had to become human to atone for the sins of humanity, but Christ also had to be God for his sacrifice to pay the penalty for all people. Consider the following verses:

> For the blood of bulls and goats cannot take away sins. So when he came into the world, he said, "Sacrifice and offering you did not desire, but a body you prepared for me. Whole burnt offerings and sin-offerings you took no delight in. Then I said, 'Here I am: I have come—it is written of me in the scroll of the book—to do your will, O God.'"
> Hebrews 10:4-7

> Therefore, since the children share in flesh and blood, he likewise shared in their humanity, so that through death he could destroy the one who holds the power of death (that is, the devil)
> Hebrews 2:14

2. The Son had to become a human to relate to us as a faithful high priest.

As a human high priest that has been tempted like us, he can sympathize with and minister to humanity. Hebrews 2:17 says:

> Therefore he had to be made like his brothers and sisters in every respect, so that he could become a merciful and faithful high priest in things relating to God, to make atonement for the sins of the people.

3. The Son had to become human to become our perfect model.

Consider the following verses:

> You should have the same attitude toward one another that Christ Jesus had,
> Philippians 2:5

> keeping our eyes fixed on Jesus, the pioneer and perfecter of our faith. For the joy set out for him he endured the cross, disregarding its shame, and has taken his seat at the right hand of the throne of God. Think of him who endured such opposition against himself by sinners, so that you may not grow weary in your souls and give up.
> Hebrews 12:2-3

> For to this you were called, since Christ also suffered for you, leaving an example for you to follow in his steps. He committed no sin nor was

deceit found in his mouth. When he was maligned, he did not answer back; when he suffered, he threatened no retaliation, but committed himself to God who judges justly.
1 Peter 2:21-23

Christ being our perfect model is amplified by the fact that he limited the use of his divine attributes in the incarnation. Otherwise, we might simply say, "Oh, Jesus is God, and therefore, we can't do this or that!" However, Christ had to wake up in the morning to pray in order to discern God's guidance (Is 50:4, Mk 1:35). He had to pray all night to discern which disciples to appoint as his apostles (Lk 6:12-13). He had to fast for forty days to conquer the devil and become empowered for his ministry (Lk 4:1-14). Christ lived the perfect human life, so that we could model him.

4. The Son had to become human to rule over earth.

It was God's original plan for Adam to rule the earth with his wife. In Genesis 1:28, God said this to Adam and Eve, "Be fruitful and multiply! Fill the earth and subdue it! Rule over the fish of the sea and the birds of the air and every creature that moves on the ground." However, when Adam sinned, he lost his opportunity to rule as God intended. Hebrews 2:8 describes how it was God's original intention for humanity to rule but that presently "all things" are not under man's control. The writer says: "You put all things under his control.' For when he put all things under his control, he left nothing outside of his control. At present we do not yet see all things under his control." Currently, all things are not under humanity's control, but through Christ, God's original plan will be fulfilled. Ephesians 1:22 says this in the context of Christ's resurrection and ascension, "God put all things under Christ's feet, and he gave him to the church as head over all things." Also, in

Matthew 28:18, after his resurrection, Christ said, "All authority in heaven and on earth has been given to me." This rule will be fully manifest when Christ returns to the earth, and as his body, believers will rule with him (cf. Rom 8:17, Rev 3:21, Lk 19:17, 1 Cor 6:3).

Application

How can we apply Christ's incarnation to our lives? It is good to remember that the Philippians 2:5-11 incarnation passage begins with, "Your attitude should be the same as that of Christ Jesus" (Phil 2:5). The hypostatic union, though mysterious, is meant to be a practical doctrine that affects the way we live. Therefore, it can be applied in many ways:

- Christ's incarnation challenges us to give up our rights in order to love God and others.

Philippians 2:6-7 says, "who though he existed in the form of God did not regard equality with God as something to be grasped, but emptied himself..." Christ did not hold onto his rights and privileges as deity but relinquished them in order to better love God and others. Likewise, in Romans 14:21, Paul said, "It is good not to eat meat or drink wine or to do anything that causes your brother to stumble." To love God and others better, we often will need to give up certain rights and privileges, even as Christ did in the incarnation.

- Christ's incarnation challenges us to be servants of God and others.

In Philippians 2:7, Paul said Christ "emptied himself by taking on the form of a slave, by looking like other men, and by sharing in human nature." A slave or servant is consumed with the desires of those he serves. Likewise, instead of living for himself and his comfort, Christ sought to sacrificially serve God and others with his life. Mark 10:45 says, "For even the Son of Man did not come to be served but to serve, and to give his life as a ransom for many."

Similarly, Paul said he became a slave to all to be a blessing to others. In 1 Corinthians 9:19 (NIV), he said, "Though I am free and belong to no one, I have made myself a slave to everyone, to win as many as possible." Christ served others so they might be saved, and Paul did the same. Therefore, the incarnation reminds us to live as servants—putting the salvation of the lost, the spiritual growth of believers, and the honor of God before our own desires.

- Christ's incarnation challenges us to radical obedience.

Christ's incarnation was not simply his own idea, it was God the Father's. God planned that Christ would come to earth as a human to die for humans. John 3:16 says, "For this is the way God loved the world: He gave his one and only Son..." Also, Philippians 2:8 says this about Christ's obedience, "He humbled himself, by becoming obedient to the point of death—even death on a cross!" Christ incarnated so he could live a perfect life and die as the perfect sacrifice for humanity—all in obedience to God.

Likewise, we must be willing to obey God even when he calls us to do something radical—like risking a promotion or our jobs in general to keep our integrity, sacrificing finances or comfortability to serve someone struggling, changing our career to go into ministry, or leaving our home and country to preach the gospel in a foreign land.

31

The incarnation of Christ—him being God and yet becoming human—though mysterious, is intensely practical. We must apply its principles to our lives daily.

Reflection

1. What stood out most in the reading and why?
2. Why was it necessary for Christ to be fully God and fully human (the hypostatic union)?
3. In what ways did Christ "empty himself" in his incarnation?
4. What are some ways that the incarnation can be applied practically to daily life?
5. What other questions or applications did you take from the reading?

Christ's Sinless Life

What's another important aspect of Christ's humanity? Certainly, we must consider his sinless life. He lived a perfect life without sin. Many Scriptures support this truth:

> God made the one who did not know sin to be sin for us, so that in him we would become the righteousness of God. 2 Corinthians 5:21

> And you know that Jesus was revealed to take away sins, and in him there is no sin.
> 1 John 3:5

> For we do not have a high priest incapable of sympathizing with our weaknesses, but one who has been tempted in every way just as we are, yet without sin.
> Hebrews 4:15

How can Christ be tempted in every way like us? There are two primary views on this:

1. A minority view is that Christ had a fallen nature like all humans but never sinned.

Karl Barth took this position. He said:

There must be no weakening or obscuring of the saving truth that the nature which God assumed in Christ is identical with our nature as we see it in the light of Fall. If it were otherwise, how could Christ be really like us? What concern would we have with him? We stand before God characterized by the Fall. God's Son not only assumed our nature but he entered the concrete form of our nature, under which we stand before God as men damned and lost.[8]

Also, T.F. Torrance said this:

His taking of our flesh of sin was a sinless action, which means that Jesus does not do in the flesh of sin what we do, namely, sin, but it also means that by remaining holy and sinless in our flesh, he condemned sin in the flesh he assumed and judged it by his very sinlessness.[9]

This would mean that Christ not only conquered temptations from Satan and the world, but also temptations from a fallen nature (an inner tendency towards sin), which he received from Mary. Certainly, this would fit the writer's statement in Hebrews that Christ was "tempted in every way just as we are, yet without sin" (4:15). Our temptations are not primarily from the world and Satan, but from our flesh (Jam 1:14). This would demonstrate how great Christ's victory over temptation was and, therefore, how he can relate to us and minister to us.

Those who take this view would use Romans 8:3 and Philippians 2:7 as support.[10] Romans 8:3 says, "For God achieved what the law could not do because it was weakened through the flesh. By sending his own Son in the likeness of sinful flesh and concerning sin, he condemned sin in the flesh." They would argue that when Paul says Christ came "in the likeness of sinful flesh," he was not simply saying Christ was "similar" to humans who have a sinful nature, but that he was just like them—a human who had a fallen nature. They would point to Philippians 2:7 (NIV) which says, Christ was "made in human likeness." Clearly, the word "likeness" used in that context is not arguing for Christ being similar to humans but actually being one. Since the same Greek word for "likeness" is used in both texts about Christ (Rom 8:3 and Phil 2:7), proponents of this view argue that the word should be interpreted the same. Christ came in the likeness of sinful flesh in that he was like humans in every way, including having a sinful nature (though never sinning).

With that said, there are logical complications with this view, such as: since sacrifices had to be without blemish (Dt 17:1), can Christ's sacrifice be considered unblemished and therefore acceptable to God if he had a sin nature (Heb 9:14)? In addition, if Christ had Adam's sin nature, he also was under Adam's guilt, as all humans are. Romans 5:12 says, "So then, just as sin entered the world through one man and death through sin, and so death spread to all people because all sinned." All humans "sinned" in Adam and consequently die, including babies who have never intentionally sinned. Therefore, could Christ's death be salvific for all people if his death, at least in part, was a just consequence of Adam's sin? Because of these complications and others, many have struggled with accepting this view.[11]

2. The predominant view historically is that Christ had a perfect nature, like Adam, but never sinned.

According to this view, Christ was tempted by the world and Satan but never from a fallen nature. Support for this view is reflected in Christ being called the last Adam. First Corinthians 15:22, 45 says: "For just as in Adam all die, so also in Christ all will be made alive... So also it is written, 'The first man, Adam, became a living person'; the last Adam became a life-giving spirit."

Being the last Adam implies that Christ came like Adam did—without a sinful nature. Where Adam fell when tempted by Satan, Christ did not. Adam led his offspring into sin and death; while Christ led his offspring (those who come to him in faith) into righteousness and eternal life.

How did Christ avoid a sinful nature, though he was born of a woman? Traditionally, it has often been said that since Christ did not have a human father, he did not inherit a fallen nature. However, humanity's sin nature is inherited from being in Adam's line, which includes both mother and father. Scripture never teaches that fathers pass on the sin nature and not mothers. Christ not having a sin nature is probably best attributed to the fact that the Holy Spirit shielded him from it at conception (Lk 1:35).

How then could Christ be tempted in "every way" like us (Heb 4:15)? In "every way" would mean he was tempted by the same temptations—like lust, anger, unbelief, and fear—though not from the same avenues. He was tempted by Satan and the world but not through the flesh. Either way, Christ's experience of human temptations makes him able to sympathize with us.

With that said, some find Christ's ability to sympathize with us incredulous. They say, "How can he sympathize with us if he has never been tempted by the flesh or fallen to temptation—never lied or been sinfully angry? How can he relate to us without those experiences?"

Consider this illustration: Two Olympic powerlifters had to deadlift a heavy weight over their head for five seconds. One person lifted the weight but only for one second and then dropped it. The second lifted the weight and held it for the complete five seconds. If we were aspiring, competitive powerlifters, who would we ask for help? Obviously, we would ask the person who held the weight without dropping it. That is true of our Savior. Christ bore the full weight of temptation without failing, and because he never failed, he bore more temptation than any other human. Therefore, he can not only sympathize with us but help us in our time of need.

John MacArthur's comments on this are helpful:

> There is a degree of temptation that we may never experience simply because, no matter what our spirituality, we will succumb before we reach it. But Jesus Christ had no such limitation. Since He was sinless, He took the full extent of all that Satan could throw at Him. He had no shock system, no weakness limit, to turn off temptation at a certain point. Since He never succumbed, He experienced every temptation to the maximum. And He experienced it as a man, as a human being. In every way He was tempted as we are, and more. The only difference was that He never sinned. Therefore, when we come to Jesus Christ we can remember that He knows everything we know, and a great deal that we do not know, about temptation, and testing, and pain. We do not have a high priest who cannot sympathize with our weaknesses.[12]

Reflection

1. What stood out most in the reading and why?
2. Why was it important for Christ to be sinless?
3. What are supports for Christ having a fallen nature but never sinning?
4. What are supports for Christ having a nature like pre-fall Adam but never sinning?
5. Which view do you think Scripture best supports?
6. What other questions or applications did you take from the reading?

Christ's Death

Scripture teaches that Christ died as an atoning sacrifice for mankind. To "atone" means to pay the penalty for sins. Two reasons are given in Scripture for Christ's atoning death—God's love and his justice.[13] John 3:16 speaks of God's love. "For this is the way God loved the world: He gave his one and only Son, so that everyone who believes in him will not perish but have eternal life." Because God loved people, he sent his Son to die for them. However, God also sent his Son to die because he is just, and therefore, sin must be punished. Romans 6:23 (NIV) says "the wages of sin is death." Also, Hebrews 9:22 says, "without the shedding of blood there is no forgiveness." Christ died to pay the wages of sin so that sinners could be forgiven by a just God. Isaiah 53:5 prophesied this about Christ. It says: "He was wounded because of our rebellious deeds, crushed because of our sins; he endured punishment that made us well; because of his wounds we have been healed." In addition, John said this:

> and he himself is the atoning sacrifice for our sins, and not only for our sins but also for the whole world.
> 1 John 2:2

> But if we walk in the light as he himself is in the light, we have fellowship with one another and the blood of Jesus his Son cleanses us from all sin.

1 John 1:7

But not only did Christ die for our sins, he gave us his perfect righteousness (cf. 1 Cor 1:30, Phil 3:9, Rom 5:19). This is the doctrine of imputation. To "impute" means to credit something to the account of another. Scripture teaches that on the cross, our sin was imputed to Christ's account, and when we, by faith, accept Christ as our Lord and Savior, his righteous life is accounted to ours. Therefore, there is a double imputation. Second Corinthians 5:21 says, "God made the one who did not know sin to be sin for us, so that in him we would become the righteousness of God."

On the cross, our sins were imputed to Christ, and consequently, God's wrath was poured out on him. As Christ bore our sins and God's wrath for them on the cross, he atoned for our sins—he made amends for our failures by paying the penalty for them.

The Extent of the Atonement

Who did Christ atone for? What is the scope of his atoning death? There are two primary views on this: One is called limited atonement. It teaches that Christ's atonement was limited in that it paid the penalty for the sins of the elect (Eph 1:4)—those chosen by God before the foundation of the earth who will eventually accept Christ—but not for the sins of unbelievers who will ultimately reject him. The argument is, "If Christ paid for the sins of the whole world, then why would anybody go to hell?"

There are many passages that teach Christ died specifically for believers. John 10:11 says: "I am the good shepherd. The good shepherd lays down his life for the sheep." Who are the sheep that Christ died for? Sheep refer to believers. Ephesians 5:25 says, "Husbands, love your wives just as Christ loved the church and gave himself for her." Who did Christ give his life for? The church.

The limited atonement view is common among those from reformed backgrounds such as Presbyterians and Reformed Baptists. Again, this view helps answer the question, "How come unbelievers go to hell if Christ paid for the sins of everyone?" Proponents of this view see it guarding against a liberal view called universalism, which teaches that everybody will ultimately go to heaven, which clearly is not supported in Scripture (cf. Rev 20:11-15).

With that said, the weakness of the limited atonement view is that Scripture never says Christ did not die for all people. And, there are many Scriptures that at least seem to indicate that Christ died for every person and not just for those who would accept him. Here are a few:

> and he himself is the atoning sacrifice for our sins, and not only for our sins but also for the whole world.
> 1 John 2:2

> But false prophets arose among the people, just as there will be false teachers among you. These false teachers will infiltrate your midst with destructive heresies, even to the point of denying the Master who bought them. As a result, they will bring swift destruction on themselves.
> 2 Peter 2:1

> For this is the way God loved the world: He gave his one and only Son, so that everyone who believes in him will not perish but have eternal life.
> John 3:16

This is the view that most believers hold, and it is called "unlimited atonement" or "general atonement." This means that Christ not only paid for the sins of believers but also for those who will ultimately reject him. However, it must be noted, that even those who believe in unlimited atonement would say the atonement is limited in some way, since everybody will not be saved. They would say Christ died to pay for the sins of the world, but the payment is applied only to those who repent and follow Christ. Therefore, the atonement is universal but limited in application.

As a contemporary illustration, it is possible to purchase gifts for everyone at a party, and yet only a few take the gift, while most leave it behind. Some might not like the gift; others would prefer to buy their own. Some might have forgotten about the gift, and others might not have heard that there was a free gift. Only those who knew about the gift and chose to accept it, received the gift. Likewise, Christ died for the sins of every person on the earth, so they can have salvation (reconciliation with God), but only a few will receive it. Romans 6:23 says, "For the payoff of sin is death, but the gift of God is eternal life in Christ Jesus our Lord."

Christ's Time in the Grave

What did Christ do while he was in the grave? Like the extent of the atonement, there is some controversy over exactly what Christ did while his body was in the grave. Some believe Christ's spirit went to heaven for three days, while others believe he went to a place called sheol, a temporary abode for the dead in the center of the earth, often mentioned in the Old Testament (Gen 37:35, Ps 16:10, 86:13, Ecc 9:10, Hosea 13:14, Job 14:13, 26:6, etc.). Sheol is a general term, which can be translated as "grave" or "realm of the dead."[14]

The crux of the argument is based on Christ's words to the thief who was on the cross next to him. In Luke 23:43, Christ said,

"I tell you the truth, today you will be with me in paradise." The question is, "Where was paradise?" Paradise is clearly a place of blessing where the righteous go after death. Revelation 2:10 and 1 Corinthians 12:2-4 use the word as a synonym for heaven.

However, even though the righteous and ungodly have always gone to separate places, many believe that before Christ's resurrection, those two places were separate sections in sheol. The place for the righteous was called paradise (or Abraham's side), and the place for the ungodly was called hell. Between these two places was a "great chasm" which no one could cross (Lk 16:26). This great chasm indicated that after death, a person's fate was sealed and could not be changed.[15] These two places in sheol are referred to in Christ's story about a poor man named Lazarus and a rich man. In Luke 16:22-26, Christ said:

> Now the poor man died and was carried by the angels to Abraham's side. The rich man also died and was buried. And in hell, as he was in torment, he looked up and saw Abraham far off with Lazarus at his side. So he called out, 'Father Abraham, have mercy on me, and send Lazarus to dip the tip of his finger in water and cool my tongue, because I am in anguish in this fire.' But Abraham said, 'Child, remember that in your lifetime you received your good things and Lazarus likewise bad things, but now he is comforted here and you are in anguish. Besides all this, a great chasm has been fixed between us, so that those who want to cross over from here to you cannot do so, and no one can cross from there to us.'

This story is a strong support for Christ's visiting paradise, which was in sheol, within the center of the earth. Those who reject this say Christ's story was a parable—a fictional story given to teach a spiritual principle. However, what makes this story unique is that Christ uses names, which never happen in parables. Christ speaks of Abraham (a real person) and a poor man named Lazarus. Using the names of real people instead of, for example, the "older brother" and "younger brother" in the Parable of the Prodigal Son, gives credence that the story was an actual event, including paradise being within sheol.

Further support that Christ went to the center of the earth after his death is Ephesians 4:8-9:

> Therefore it says, "When he ascended on high he captured captives; he gave gifts to men." Now what is the meaning of "he ascended," except that he also descended to the lower regions, namely, the earth?

Before Christ's ascension into heaven, he first descended to the lower regions. This certainly refers to the incarnation, Christ coming to earth generally. But the description of "lower, earthly regions" (NIV) could also refer to (or include) his time in sheol, right before his ascension (cf. Matt 12:40).

Finally, support for Christ's time in sheol can be found in 1 Peter 3:18-20, which says:

> Because Christ also suffered once for sins, the just for the unjust, to bring you to God, by being put to death in the flesh but by being made alive in the spirit. In it he went and preached to the spirits in prison, after they were disobedient long ago when God patiently waited in the days of Noah as an ark was being constructed. In the ark a few, that is eight souls, were delivered through water.

Though this is a controversial text, many believe it refers to Christ being in paradise proclaiming his victory over demon spirits held captive in hell. These spirits would be those who mated with women before the flood—creating a super race (Gen 6:1-4). Jude 1:6 describes them: "You also know that the angels who did not keep within their proper domain but abandoned their own place of residence, he has kept in eternal chains in utter darkness, locked up for the judgment of the great Day." Likewise, Colossians 2:15 may describe Christ's public proclamation of victory over these demons in sheol. It says, "Disarming the rulers and authorities, he has made a public disgrace of them, triumphing over them by the cross."

Apparently, paradise, and the believers in it, were moved to heaven after Christ's resurrection. Ephesians 4:8 may refer to this when it says, "When he ascended on high he captured captives." When ancient kings defeated an enemy, they would not only take enemy prisoners and lead them through their own cities in a victory parade as trophies, but also commonly recapture their own soldiers, who were previously taken as prisoners.[16] When Christ ascended from sheol to heaven, he took his own people to heaven with him. This was the view of the early church. John MacArthur said this about the early church's belief:

> Early church dogma taught that the righteous dead of the Old Testament could not be taken into the fullness of God's presence until Christ had purchased their redemption on the cross, and that they had waited in this place for His victory on that day. Figuratively speaking, the early church Fathers said that, after announcing His triumph over demons in one part of Sheol, He then opened the doors of another part of Sheol to release those godly captives. Like the victorious kings of old, He recaptured the captives and liberated them, and henceforth they would live in heaven as eternally free sons of God.[17]

46

With all this said, it must be noted that there is no support for Christ suffering for our sins in hell. Scripture teaches that Christ's death was sufficient to pay the penalty of our sins (cf. 1 Cor 15:3, Heb 10:12)—no further suffering was needed. When he went to sheol, his time was spent in paradise—the place of the righteous. There he declared his victory over the enemy (Col 2:15) and then took the righteous to heaven (Eph 4:8).

Reflection

1. What stood out most in the reading and why?
2. What is limited atonement and what are supports for that view?
3. What is unlimited atonement and what are supports for that view?
4. Which view of atonement do you think Scripture best supports?
5. Where did Christ go while in the grave and what did he do there? What scriptures support your view?
6. What other questions or applications did you take from the reading?

Christ's Resurrection

Christ's resurrection is an essential aspect of the gospel and our Christian faith. In Romans 10:9, Paul said, "… if you confess with your mouth that Jesus is Lord and believe in your heart that God raised him from the dead, you will be saved." Likewise, in 1 Corinthians 15:3-4, Paul describes the resurrection, as well as other fundamentals of the gospel, as of "first importance." In 1 Corinthians 15:14 and 17 (ESV) Paul taught that if Christ has not been raised from the dead, our "faith is in vain" and "futile." There is no Christian faith apart from the resurrection.

Its importance is demonstrated throughout the New Testament. The Gospels give testimony to the resurrection. In Acts, the apostles proclaim it throughout the world. The Epistles assume a resurrected, ruling Christ. And, Revelation predicts his coming to rule on the earth. As Wayne Grudem said, "the entire New Testament bears witness to the resurrection of Christ."[18]

Therefore, we must ask, "Why is the resurrection so important and what are its implications for the Christian life?" There are many crucial implications:

Christ's Resurrection Ensures Our New Birth

In John 3:3 (ESV), Christ said that in order to enter God's kingdom, we must be "born again." By nature, we are dead in our sins (Eph 2:1). Romans 6:23 (NIV) says, "the wages of sin is

48

death." Death refers to separation. People are separated from God as a penalty of their sins, and if never born again, they will be separated from God eternally. Spiritually speaking we are dead to God and the things of God, which is why we need to be born again. We need new life.

In Scripture, our receiving this new life is attributed in part to Christ's resurrection. First Peter 1:3 says, "Blessed be the God and Father of our Lord Jesus Christ! By his great mercy he gave us new birth into a living hope through the resurrection of Jesus Christ from the dead." In Ephesians 2:5-6, Paul said something similar: "even though we were dead in transgressions, [God] made us alive together with Christ—by grace you are saved!—and he raised us up with him and seated us with him in the heavenly realms in Christ Jesus."

When a believer accepts Christ as Lord and Savior, they are identified with Christ in his death and resurrection. Romans 6:4 says, "Therefore we have been buried with him through baptism into death, in order that just as Christ was raised from the dead through the glory of the Father, so we too may live a new life." Christ's resurrection delivers believers from spiritual death (and one day, physical death).

When somebody is physically dead, they have no sensitivity to stimuli. They can no longer enjoy or respond to beautiful music, a gentle breeze, or powerful words. This is also true of those who are spiritually dead in sin. They cannot respond to God, his Word, or worship; but when they are born again, they inherit spiritual life and therefore sensitivity to the things of God. They become hungry to know God, worship him, serve him, and others. They are spiritually equipped to worship God throughout eternity. This is what happens to a person at the new birth. In Scripture, the believer's new birth is attributed to being spiritually resurrected from the dead through identification with Christ's resurrection (1 Pet 1:3, Eph 2:5-6).

Christ's Resurrection Ensures Our Justification

In Romans 4:25 (NIV), Paul said this about Christ, "He was delivered over to death for our sins and was raised to life for our justification." Christ's resurrection was basically a declaration of God's approval. It was a divine guarantee, a receipt of payment—proving that God accepted Christ's sacrifice for sin.[19] Therefore, those who trust in Christ are justified—meaning they are declared righteous, as though they never sinned. Wayne Grudem said it this way:

> By raising Christ from the dead, God the Father was in effect saying that he approved of Christ's work of suffering and dying for our sins, that his work was completed, and that Christ no longer had any need to remain dead. There was no penalty left to pay for sin, no more wrath of God to bear, no more guilt or liability to punishment—all had been completely paid for, and no guilt remained. In the resurrection, God was saying to Christ, "I approve of what you have done, and you find favor in my sight."[20]

Remembering that we have been justified is especially important when the enemy comes to condemn us because of our sins and failures. Romans 8:1 says, "There is therefore now no condemnation for those who are in Christ Jesus." God doesn't accept us for our righteous works, whether in salvation or in sanctification. He accepts us because of Christ's righteous works (2 Cor 5:21). Therefore, we can always run into God's arms, accept his forgiveness, and enjoy his intimacy. Christ's resurrection is a proof that God accepted Christ's payment for all our sins—past, present, and future. Certainly, this isn't an excuse to live in sin. It should be a motivation to run from it (cf. Rom 6:1-4). Romans 2:4 says, "God's kindness leads you to repentance."

Christ's Resurrection Empowers Us to Conquer Sin and Live Righteously

In Christ's death, he paid the penalty for our sins and broke the power of sin over our lives. But, through the resurrection, Christ empowers us to live righteously. In Romans 6:4, 6, and 11-13, Paul says:

> Therefore we have been buried with him through baptism into death, in order that just as Christ was raised from the dead through the glory of the Father, so we too may live a new life... We know that our old man was crucified with him so that the body of sin would no longer dominate us, so that we would no longer be enslaved to sin... So you too consider yourselves dead to sin, but alive to God in Christ Jesus. Therefore do not let sin reign in your mortal body so that you obey its desires, and do not present your members to sin as instruments to be used for unrighteousness, but present yourselves to God as those who are alive from the dead and your members to God as instruments to be used for righteousness.

Being dead to sin doesn't mean that we no longer have a sin nature (v. 11)—we do. However, we are no longer slaves to that nature (v. 6). Because of Christ's resurrection, we have been empowered by God's Spirit to "live a new life" (v. 4). One day when we die and go to heaven or when we receive our glorified bodies, we will be delivered from the presence of sin all together. However, until then, we must walk in the resurrection power, which comes from Christ, to conquer sin and live righteously. In Ephesians 1:18-

51

20 (ESV), Paul prays for us to be aware of this resurrection power at work in us. He says,

> having the eyes of your hearts enlightened, that you may know … what is the immeasurable greatness of his power toward us who believe, according to the working of his great might that he worked in Christ when he raised him from the dead and seated him at his right hand in the heavenly places

But not only do we need to know the power of the resurrection in our lives, we must also access it (cf. Eph 3:16, Phil 3:10). We do this by abiding in Christ. In John 15:5, Christ said, "I am the vine; you are the branches. The one who remains in me—and I in him—bears much fruit, because apart from me you can accomplish nothing." If we're not abiding in Christ through daily prayer, Bible reading, worship, obedience to God, fellowship with the body, and serving, we won't produce much fruit. The resurrection power won't operate in our lives as it should. We'll find ourselves constantly falling to sin and temptation and unmotivated to serve God. In fact, apart from abiding, we can't do anything truly honoring to God.

Through his death and resurrection, Christ conquered sin, and because we are identified with both in our salvation (Rom 6:4), we are also empowered to conquer sin and live righteously (Rom 6:11-13). In light of this, Tony Evans said:

> Therefore, if you and I have sin in our lives that is overcoming us and beating us down, it is because we have adopted faulty thinking. We are living as if Christ's resurrection life within us is theoretical and not real. The analogy is this. If death is real and not just theoretical, then your new life in Christ and your new power over sin are real

and not theoretical. If you will learn to identify with your new life in Christ (Ephesians 2:5), rather than with your old life in Adam, you will have new victory in Christ rather than old defeat in Adam. You and I need to learn to think in terms of, "I am not what I used to be, so I don't have to act like I used to act."[21]

Likewise, in the context of speaking about Christ's resurrection and our future resurrection, Paul said this in 1 Corinthians 15:58, "So then, dear brothers and sisters, be firm. Do not be moved! Always be outstanding in the work of the Lord, knowing that your labor is not in vain in the Lord." We should stand firm in the face of all trials, including persecution, death, temptation, and failure. We must not only stand firm but endeavor to serve the Lord wholeheartedly. Christ's resurrection empowers us to conquer sin and live righteously.

Christ's Resurrection Ensures Our Future Resurrection

In Scripture, Christ's resurrection is commonly linked with the believers' future resurrection. Consider a few verses:

But now Christ has been raised from the dead, the firstfruits of those who have fallen asleep.
1 Corinthians 15:20

But our citizenship is in heaven—and we also await a savior from there, the Lord Jesus Christ, who will transform these humble bodies of ours into the likeness of his glorious body by means of that power by which he is able to subject all things to himself.
Philippians 3:20-21

Beloved, we are God's children now, and what we will be has not yet appeared; but we know that when he appears we shall be like him, because we shall see him as he is.
1 John 3:1

Christ is called the firstfruits of those who have died (1 Cor 15:20) because, like the firstfruits of a harvest, his body pictures what the future harvest will be like, when those who follow him are resurrected.[22] As Paul and John said (Phil 3:21, 1 John 3:1), our bodies will then be like his.

Since our glorified bodies will be like Christ's, we must ponder, "What is Christ's glorified body like?" Charles Ryrie notes several characteristics:

Christ's resurrection body had links with His unresurrected earthly body. People recognized Him (John 20:20), the wounds inflicted by crucifixion were retained (20:25–29; Rev. 5:6), He had the capacity (though not the need) to eat (Luke 24:30–33, 41–43), He breathed on the disciples (John 20:22), and that body had flesh and bones proving that He was not merely a spirit showing itself (Luke 24:39–40).

But His resurrection body was different. He could enter closed rooms without opening doors (Luke 24:36; John 20:19), He could appear and disappear at will (Luke 24:15; John 20:19), and apparently He was never limited by physical needs such as sleep or food.[23]

In 1 Corinthians 15:37-38, Paul compares the glory of our new bodies with the difference between a seed sown into the ground and the plant which eventually comes from it. This clarifies that our glorified bodies will not be totally new in the sense of being made out of previously nonexistent material; they will, in fact, come from our natural bodies. As Paul said, the seed of our bodies, which will be sown into the ground, will be raised "imperishable," "in glory," and "in power" (1 Cor 15:42-43). They will be made fit for the kingdom, as they will no longer age, die, or decay (1 Cor 15:50). They will be glorious, just like our Lord's body.

Conclusion

Christ's resurrection is crucial to our faith. Because of it, we are born again, justified, sanctified, and glorified. Christ's resurrection power resides in believers, enabling them to conquer sin and live righteously, and one day, through it, God will resurrect and glorify our natural bodies (cf. Rom 8:11). Apart from Christ's resurrection, our faith is in vain and futile (1 Cor 15:14, 17). Thank you, Lord, for the resurrection!

Reflection

1. What stood out most in the reading and why?
2. Why is Christ's resurrection so important for our faith?
3. What are some applications of Christ's resurrection for Christian living?
4. What other questions or applications did you take from the reading?

Christ's Ascension

After he had said this, while they were watching, he was lifted up and a cloud hid him from their sight. As they were still staring into the sky while he was going, suddenly two men in white clothing stood near them and said, "Men of Galilee, why do you stand here looking up into the sky? This same Jesus who has been taken up from you into heaven will come back in the same way you saw him go into heaven."
Acts 1:9-11

After Christ's resurrection, he stayed on the earth for forty days (Acts 1:3)—appearing to his disciples and 500 other believers (1 Cor 15:6) and encouraging them to wait for the promised Holy Spirit. Apparently, the Holy Spirit could not come until Christ ascended. In John 16:7, Christ said: "But I tell you the truth, it is to your advantage that I am going away. For if I do not go away, the Advocate will not come to you, but if I go, I will send him to you." When Christ lived on the earth, he was limited by locality. He couldn't be with each disciple at all times. However, because of Christ's ascension, every disciple is indwelled by the Holy Spirit and can experience his power, wisdom, and presence at all times.

Soon after encouraging the disciples to wait for the Spirit, Christ ascended to heaven (Acts 1:9), where he now sits at the Father's right hand until he returns to rule the earth. Hebrews 10:12

says, "But when this priest had offered for all time one sacrifice for sins, he sat down at the right hand of God." Christ's sitting represents his completion of redemption. With that said, Christ's sitting does not mean he is idle; in fact, he is still busy doing ministry for us.

Present Ministry

What is Christ's present ministry in heaven?

1. In heaven, Christ rules as Lord, at the right hand of God, and is awaiting his ultimate rule.

In Acts 2:34-36, Peter said this (as he quoted Psalm 110:1):

For David did not ascend into heaven, but he himself says, 'The Lord said to my lord, "Sit at my right hand until I make your enemies a footstool for your feet."' Therefore let all the house of Israel know beyond a doubt that God has made this Jesus whom you crucified both Lord and Christ.

Christ currently rules at the right hand of God. When Christ commissioned the disciples, he described this, as he said that all authority in heaven and earth had been given to him (Matt 28:18). Christ's rule in heaven includes the restoration of his former glory. In John 17:5, Christ prayed, "And now, Father, glorify me at your side with the glory I had with you before the world was created." In addition, his rule includes forming, leading, gifting, empowering, and ministering to the church as its Head (cf. Mk 1:8, Col 1:18, Eph 4:7-13, John 15:1-10, 5:23-31). Ephesians 5:23 says, "For the husband is the head of the wife even as Christ is the head of the church, his body, and is himself its Savior."

At the right hand of God, Christ awaits the time when God will bring all into submission, as Christ's enemies become his "footstool" (Heb 10:13). This will ultimately happen at Christ's return when he judges those who reject him and rewards the faithful. Christ said that the Father judged no one but had entrusted judgment to Christ (John 5:22). Christ will judge unbelievers at the great white throne of judgment (Rev 20:11-15) and believers at the judgment seat of Christ (2 Cor 5:21). Ultimately, every knee will bow and every tongue will confess Christ as Lord (Phil 2:10-11). Currently, Christ rules in the heavens as Lord until he returns to rule on earth.

What else does Christ do in his present ministry?

2. In heaven, Christ intercedes for all believers as their high priest.

As high priest, Christ represents believers before God—praying for God to forgive their sins and keep them from the evil one, for them to be sanctified and united, among other things (cf. John 17). Since Christ is both human and God, he can relate to his people and sympathize with them in their weakness. Hebrews 4:15-16 says:

> For we do not have a high priest incapable of sympathizing with our weaknesses, but one who has been tempted in every way just as we are, yet without sin. Therefore let us confidently approach the throne of grace to receive mercy and find grace whenever we need help.

He understands being hungry, lonely, rejected, hated, criticized, and tempted. Therefore, with this understanding, he intercedes for believers, including keeping them from ultimately falling away from God. Hebrews 7:24-25 says, "but he holds his priesthood permanently since he lives forever. So he is able to save completely those who come to God through him, because he always lives to intercede for them."

Certainly, we get a good picture of Christ's intercession in how he prayed for Peter right before Peter denied Christ. In Luke 22:31-32, Christ said, "Simon, Simon, pay attention! Satan has demanded to have you all, to sift you like wheat, but I have prayed for you, Simon, that your faith may not fail. When you have turned back, strengthen your brothers." No doubt, Christ prays for us as we encounter temptations as well—that our faith would grow through the trial, that we would remain faithful to the Lord, and ultimately strengthen other believers.

3. In heaven, Christ is preparing a perfect, eternal abode for his people.

In John 14:1-3, Christ said this to his disciples who were discouraged about his leaving:

> Do not let your hearts be distressed. You believe in God; believe also in me. There are many dwelling places in my Father's house. Otherwise, I would have told you, because I am going away to make ready a place for you. And if I go and make ready a place for you, I will come again and take you to be with me, so that where I am you may be too.

Revelation 21:2 describes the "place" Christ has prepared for believers when it says, "And I saw the holy city—the new Jerusalem—descending out of heaven from God, made ready like a bride adorned for her husband." As heavenly Jerusalem descends to the earth, we can be sure it is our Lord who has made her "ready." This gives us hope. Christ will return, and we will dwell with him eternally in our perfect abode (cf. Rev 21:9-22:5).

Application

How should Christ's present, heavenly ministry encourage us?

1. Christ's heavenly ministry should encourage us to pray.

If Christ, as our high priest, continually intercedes for believers (Heb 7:25), then certainly we should continually pray for them as well. We should pray that God would sanctify, protect, and use believers to build God's kingdom (cf. John 17).

In addition, since Christ awaits his ultimate kingdom and rule on the earth, we should continually pray for his kingdom to come, as taught in the Lord's Prayer (Matt 6:12). This includes praying for the salvation of the lost, the spread of peace, righteousness, and joy throughout the earth (Rom 14:17), Christ's return, the judgment of the lost, and the rewarding of the saints.

2. Christ's heavenly ministry should assure us of the believers' eternal security.

Though there are many texts calling believers to persevere in the faith, and that only those who persevere in the faith are truly saved (cf. Col 1:22-23, Matt 24:13), ultimately, this perseverance is enabled by Christ. He is the one who seals us with the Holy Spirit (Eph 4:30), prays for us so we can be saved to the uttermost (Heb 7:25), protects us in the midst of trials and temptations (1 Cor 10:13), and puts us in his hand (and the Father's hand) to keep us (John 10:28-29). Our ultimate salvation depends on Christ, who will keep every true believer. He came to do the Father's will, and God's will is that Christ lose none of the elect but that he would raise them up in the last days (John 6:38-39).

3. Christ's heavenly ministry should encourage us in our ministry, as we understand the authority and power we have in him.

Since believers are unified with Christ in his redemption (in his death, burial, and resurrection, Rom 6:3-5; cf. 1 Cor 12:13), we are also unified with him in his ascension. This seems to be what Paul refers to in Ephesians 2:6 when he said, "and he raised us up with him and seated us with him in the heavenly realms in Christ Jesus." And since his ascension is associated with authority and power to rule (Eph 1:20-23), believers have a measure of authority and power in Christ now and will share it more fully when Christ returns. Wayne Grudem provides further insight on this:

> But if Christ's session at God's right hand refers to his reception of authority, then the fact that God has made us sit with Christ means that we share in some measure in the authority that Christ has, authority to contend against "the spiritual hosts of wickedness in the heavenly places" (Eph. 6:12; cf. vv. 10–18) and to do battle with weapons that "have divine power to destroy strongholds" (2 Cor. 10:4)[24]

Certainly, we should take confidence in our position in Christ as we pray over individuals, communities, and nations under spiritual attack. We are seated in Christ over demonic powers and authorities (Eph 2:6, 1:20-23). Also, we should take confidence in our union with Christ when it comes to various types of ministry: counseling, administrating, preaching, and leading. The power that both raised Christ from the dead and ascended him into heaven is working in us. Paul actually prayed for our eyes to be awakened to understand this (Eph 1:17-22). Surely, Christ was encouraging the disciples with this new reality when he commissioned them to make disciples. In Matthew 28:18-19, he said, "All authority in heaven and on earth has been given to me. Therefore go and make disciples of all nations..." Christ had received this authority and power, and he was sharing it with the disciples to do ministry in his name. As we abide in Christ through prayer, worship, and time in God's Word, we tap into this authority and power to do effective ministry (John 15:4-5).

As mentioned, believers will share in Christ's authority and power more fully in the coming kingdom. In 1 Corinthians 6:2-3, Paul said, "Or do you not know that the saints will judge the world? And if the world is to be judged by you, are you not competent to settle trivial suits? Do you not know that we will judge angels? Why not ordinary matters!" Also, Christ promised this for believers in Revelation 2:26-27,

> And to the one who conquers and who continues in my deeds until the end, I will give him authority over the nations—he will rule them with an iron rod and like clay jars he will break them to pieces

Again, this should give us great confidence as we minister to others. Because of our union with Christ in his ascension, we share in his authority and power. As we abide in him, we are empowered to serve God and others more effectively. One day, we will rule and serve others with him at his coming.

4. Christ's heavenly ministry should encourage us to be patient, as we wait for his second coming.

As Christ waits at the right hand of God (cf. Heb 10:12), in this season of grace, we wait. We wait, not in the sense that we are not active in completing the great commission. We wait in the sense that we shouldn't be anxious or worried about the apparent lack of fruit or evil that surrounds us. Christ is coming and his enemies will become his footstool (Heb 10:13). All will submit to Christ and call him Lord (Phil 2:10-11). We wait patiently for this. In addition, though often not acknowledged or rewarded in this season on earth, in fact, often receiving the opposite of those things, one day Christ will return and reward those who faithfully persevered in serving him (Matt 25:21). Christ's present ministry of waiting at the right hand of God should encourage us to patiently wait for his return with our hearts, as we actively serve him with our bodies. In James 5:7-8, James encouraged suffering believers with these words:

> So be patient, brothers and sisters, until the Lord's return. Think of how the farmer waits for the precious fruit of the ground and is patient for it until it receives the early and late rains. You also be patient and strengthen your hearts, for the Lord's return is near.

Amen! Come, Lord Jesus!

Reflection

1. What stood out most in the reading and why?
2. What is Christ currently doing in heaven?
3. How should his current heavenly ministry affect our lives?
4. What other questions or applications did you take from the reading?

Evidence for Christ's Deity: His Teaching and the Resurrection

> When Jesus came to the area of Caesarea Philippi, he asked his disciples, "Who do people say that the Son of Man is?" They answered, "Some say John the Baptist, others Elijah, and others Jeremiah or one of the prophets." He said to them, "But who do you say that I am?" Simon Peter answered, "You are the Christ, the Son of the living God." And Jesus answered him, "You are blessed, Simon son of Jonah, because flesh and blood did not reveal this to you, but my Father in heaven! And I tell you that you are Peter, and on this rock I will build my church, and the gates of Hades will not overpower it.
> Matthew 16:13-18

Who was Jesus? In Matthew 16:13-18, when Jesus asked the disciples who people said he was, they gave various answers: He was a prophet, John the Baptist, the second coming of Elijah. Essentially, the answer people came up with was that Jesus was a righteous man or a good prophet.

But, when Peter was asked about Jesus' identity, he replied, "You are the Christ, the Son of the living God." Now we should understand that this was a very controversial claim, one which ultimately led to Christ's execution. Consider how the Jews responded to Christ's claim of God being his Father in John 5:17-18:

> So he told them, "My Father is working until now, and I too am working." For this reason the Jewish leaders were

trying even harder to kill him, because not only was he breaking the Sabbath, but he was also calling God his own Father, thus making himself equal with God.

Jesus claimed to be equal with God, which was blasphemous to Jews. Likewise, in John 10:30, he claimed that he and the Father were one. His followers taught this also. In John 1:1-3, John said:

> In the beginning was the Word, and the Word was with God, and the Word was fully God. The Word was with God in the beginning. All things were created by him, and apart from him not one thing was created that has been created.

The "Word" was John's favorite name for Jesus. Jesus was the very communication of God. He was with God in the beginning and was God. He created the earth. Likewise, in 2 Peter 1:1, Peter called Jesus "our God and Savior." This is what separates Christ from many other founders of religions such as Buddha and Muhammad; he claimed to be God and his followers taught the same.

Who was Jesus? Though Jesus taught that he was the Son of God and died because of it and his disciples taught the same and were persecuted for it, most today would not answer the question the way they did. Like the early Jews, they would say Jesus was a good man, a wise teacher, or a prophet but not God. For example, a secular book published by Cambridge Press in 2013 called Who's Bigger? ranked Jesus as the most significant figure in all of human history by using quantitative analysis.[25] Likewise, the Koran calls Jesus "the greatest above all in this world and in the world to come" (Imran v. 45) and describes him as "holy"—meaning without sin (Sura 19:19). However, when considering these high praises written about Jesus, both fall short of saying what Jesus and his followers said—that Jesus was God.

In this study, we will answer the question, "Was Jesus God?" We will do this by considering several evidences that point to his deity.

Jesus' Teachings as Evidence of His Deity

As mentioned, the most commonly accepted view of Jesus is that he was simply a good man, moral teacher, or prophet from God. Something we must then ask: "Are these common conclusions about who Jesus was really feasible, considering all that Jesus said and taught?" Let's reflect on a few controversial statements Jesus said:

1. Jesus' Claim of Resurrecting Himself

Hypothetically, let's say that during dinner time at a restaurant, a person stood on a table and started publicly declaring, "Shoot me! Shoot me! And, in three days I will raise myself from the dead!" What would everybody think? They would probably question, "Is this guy OK? Did he forget his medications?" People would think the man was crazy, immediately call 911, and try to get him help.

However, that scenario is very similar to something Christ did while alive. In John 2:19, he said to a crowd, "Destroy this temple [referring to his body] and in three days I will raise it up again." When considering Christ's words, it would be illogical to call Jesus a good man, or wise, moral teacher. Good, moral people don't go around encouraging people to kill them and declaring they will resurrect themselves.

2. Jesus' Claim of Forgiving Sins

66

In addition, consider another illustration about the same hypothetical man. Outside of the downtown courtroom, this man is now claiming to forgive people who have been charged with crimes. As robbers, prostitutes, and murderers are escorted to jail, the man continually says to them, "I forgive you." This would be fine if he had a personal relationship with these criminals and they had harmed him in some way, but the man doesn't know these people and hasn't been harmed by them. Only a person hurt by another can forgive his or her sins. Again, this would be strange.

However, this again mirrors something that Christ did. In the Gospel of Mark, Jesus forgave the sins of a paralytic, which angered the religious leaders who were watching. Mark 2:5-7 details this:

> When Jesus saw their faith, he said to the paralytic, "Son, your sins are forgiven." Now some of the experts in the law were sitting there, turning these things over in their minds: "Why does this man speak this way? He is blaspheming! Who can forgive sins but God alone?"

As mentioned, the religious leaders were baffled by Christ's words and considered it blasphemy. Who can forgive sins but God?

Most of us would find a person professing to forgive our sins whom we have not harmed very strange. Again, this is exactly what Christ did. Is it really possible that Christ could be a great moral teacher and say ridiculous things like this?

3. Jesus' Claim of Judging the World

In addition to the previous scenarios, this hypothetical man is now standing at a major intersection and declaring to all who pass by that he is going to judge the world—separating people like a shepherd separates sheep and goats. The sheep will go to heaven and the goats to hell. Again, wouldn't this seem strange and possibly scary? To make this even worse, this man claimed to be the Son of God and that only those who follow him are sheep who will go to heaven. Because of his teaching, many left their friends, families, and careers to follow this man.

These are all things that Christ taught and did (Matt 25:31-46, John 14:6). Is it really reasonable to accept Christ as a good man, moral teacher, or prophet from God considering his teachings? This is what C.S Lewis, a former professor at Cambridge University, said in his book Mere Christianity:

> I am trying here to prevent anyone from saying the really foolish thing that people often say about Him: I'm ready to accept Jesus as a great moral teacher, but I don't accept His claim to be God. That is one thing we must not say. A man who was merely a man and said the sort of thing Jesus said would not be a great moral teacher. He would either be a lunatic… or else he would be the Devil of Hell. You must make your choice. Either this man was and is the Son of God: or else a madman or something worse. … You can shut Him up for a fool, you can spit at Him and kill Him as a demon; or you can fall at His feet and call Him Lord and God.

It is impossible to consider what Christ said and did and yet take the common view that he was a good man, moral teacher, or prophet from God. He is either God, like he said, or he was a liar, lunatic, or demon. There is no middle ground.

What Jesus claimed and taught is an evidence for his deity. By itself, it is not very convincing, but it is an important evidence, especially for those who reject Christ's claim of deity and yet accept him as either a good man, moral teacher, or prophet from God. What Christ taught and did doesn't leave those as reasonable options.

Jesus' Resurrection as Evidence of His Deity

What are other proofs that Jesus is God? One of the greatest proofs is the historical evidence for Jesus' resurrection. In 1 Corinthians 15:14, Paul said, "And if Christ has not been raised, then our preaching is futile and your faith is empty." Without the resurrection, there is no Christian faith. It is the crux of Christianity.

What are evidences for Christ's resurrection? Specifically, there are documented eye-witness testimonies. It has often been said that there is more historical evidence for Christ's resurrection than that Julius Caesar lived.[26] In fact, Brooke Foss Westcott, a British scholar who lived from 1825-1901, said this: "Indeed taking all the evidence together, it is not too much to say that there is no historic incident better or more variously supported than the resurrection of Christ."[27] If we reject the evidence of Christ's resurrection, then we will have to reject much of what we know about ancient history. We'll consider evidences for the resurrection below.

The Case of the Empty Tomb

It is well attested historically that Christ died on the cross. Not only do we have the testimony of New Testament authors, but also ancient, secular historians like Josephus and Tacitus who recorded the event in their writings.[28] In addition, medical experts, using scientific research, have examined the circumstances of Christ's crucifixion, including the fact that he was beaten to disfigurement before his crucifixion (Is 52:14, John 19:1-3), that people crucified typically died by asphyxiation (not being able to breath), and that he was pierced by a professional executioner to confirm his death (John 19:34), and concluded that Christ couldn't have survived.[29]

After Christ's crucifixion, he was buried in a rich man's tomb. The tomb was sealed and guarded by soldiers. When Christ resurrected, there was a great earthquake, an angel appeared and rolled away the stone, and the guards ran away. Christ was no longer present in the grave, but his clothes laid on the ground (Matt 28:1-10, Mk 16:1-8, Lk 24:1-8, John 20:1-18). The empty grave was first found by some women followers, and then, they told Christ's disciples. To account for the missing body, the Pharisees accused the disciples of stealing it and paid the guards a large sum to remain quiet (Matt 28:11-15).

Since Christ, without a doubt, died and was buried, we must ask the question, "Was there really an empty tomb?" This is a fundamental question that must be answered affirmatively to prove that Christ did in fact rise from the dead. We'll consider a few evidences below:

1. Proof of an empty tomb is the fact that Christ's body was never produced as evidence against the resurrection. Paul taught that the resurrection is the crux of the Christian faith. If Christ has not been raised from the dead, our faith is in vain (1 Cor 15:14, 17). Therefore, in order to stop Christianity from growing, all the authorities had to do was prosecute the disciples (including having the soldiers testify) and produce the body. However, there is no historical record of the disciples ever being charged for stealing Christ's body.[30] Instead, the disciples were threatened to stop preaching the resurrection, flogged, jailed, exiled, and most were ultimately martyred. If the Jews had produced the body or even given an adequate explanation for the fact that it was missing, it would have

ended Christianity before it began. However, they didn't. The tomb was empty, and the body was never found.

2. Proof of an empty tomb is the fact that women were the first and primary witnesses of Christ's resurrection (Matt 28:1-10, John 20:1, 14-18). Since women had such a low standing in ancient Jewish and Roman societies, it wouldn't make sense for the disciples to fabricate a resurrection story with women witnesses. In fact, in a Jewish court of law, a woman's testimony was not even admissible.[31] If the disciples were going to fabricate a resurrection story, they would have surely chosen the initial witnesses to be male. This shows that the Gospel writers faithfully recorded what happened even if it would have been embarrassing or unconvincing in their culture.[32] When women went to see Christ's body at the tomb, it was empty. Christ had resurrected.

3. Proof of an empty tomb is the historical lack of tomb veneration. During the period Jesus lived, there were at least fifty tombs of prophets or holy persons which served as sites of religious worship and veneration.[33] With Jesus being the founder of Christianity, certainly early followers would have regularly visited his grave if his body was still there. However, there is no record of that.[34] This is further proof that the body was never found and that the tomb was empty.

The empty tomb is a necessary evidence of Christ's resurrection. What are other evidences?

The Case of the Original Apostles

A strong evidence is that of the original apostles. Who were the apostles? They were twelve devoted followers of Christ who lived and served with him during his three years of ministry. However, when Christ was betrayed by Judas (one of the twelve) and taken by the Jewish and Roman authorities to be put to death for claiming to be the messiah, they all ran away, and some denied him overtly. Though they believed in him, they were not willing to die with him.

While the disciples served Christ, he spent a considerable part of his ministry preparing them for his death. He told them that he was going to die and be raised from the dead three days later (John 2:19). He told them that the Jewish authorities were going to put him to death (Matt 16:21) and warned that they would be persecuted for following him (Matt 24:9). He even taught them that to be his disciples, they had to be willing to take up their crosses—being willing to die for their faith (Lk 14:27). However, when everything Christ taught them happened, they fled. None were willing to die with him.

With that said, this leads to one of the strongest evidences for the resurrection. After Christ rose from the dead and appeared to his apostles, each of the remaining eleven were willing to be hated, beaten, jailed, exiled, and even die for their belief. Each of the remaining eleven died for Christ—declaring that he had been resurrected—with the exception of John, who spent the last part of his life exiled on an island for prisoners because of his faith (Rev 1).

If the resurrection were not true and was simply made up, one must ask, "Why would they die for something they knew was a lie?" If the resurrection was false, surely somebody would have broken and said, "OK, OK! We lied! We stole the body and hid him!" But none did. Not only Peter, the head apostle, but also his wife died for Christ. When his wife was being taken to be crucified, he encouraged her with, "Remember the Lord!" And when it was his time to die, he requested to be crucified upside down because he didn't deserve to die like Christ. From a historical perspective, the apostle's willingness to die for their belief in the resurrection means that they truly believed it. The apostles suffering for their belief in the resurrection is a strong proof that it really happened, especially when considering that each of them fled or denied him while he was still alive.

Michael Green, Principal of St. John College, Nottingham, said this:

> [The resurrection] was the belief that turned heart broken followers of a crucified rabbi into the courageous witnesses and martyrs of the early church. This was the one belief that separated the followers of Jesus from the Jews and turned them into the community of the resurrection. You could imprison them, flog them, kill them, but you could not make them deny their conviction that on the third day he rose again.[35]

The Case of James, Jesus' Brother

Further support for the resurrection is the conversion and martyrdom of James, the brother of Jesus. During Christ's ministry, James did not believe in him, even though he witnessed the miracles. In fact, John 7:3-5 shares this about James' and Christ's other brother, Jude:

> So Jesus' brothers advised him, "Leave here and go to Judea so your disciples may see your miracles that you are performing. For no one who seeks to make a reputation for himself does anything in secret. If you are doing these things, show yourself to the world." (For not even his own brothers believed in him.)

73

However, after Christ's resurrection, he appeared to James. First Corinthians 15:3-7 says:

> For I passed on to you as of first importance what I also received—that Christ died for our sins according to the scriptures, and that he was buried, and that he was raised on the third day according to the scriptures, and that he appeared to Cephas, then to the twelve. Then he appeared to more than five hundred of the brothers and sisters at one time, most of whom are still alive, though some have fallen asleep. Then he appeared to James, then to all the apostles.

After seeing the resurrected Christ, James converted. He not only became a follower of Christ but also an apostle—an official witness of the resurrection. He became the leader of the Jerusalem church (Acts 15:13-21) and was known as "James the Just" because of his righteous character. Tradition says his knees were hard like a camel's knees because of the callouses developed from long periods in prayer.

James even wrote his own epistle which begins with "From James, a slave of God and the Lord Jesus Christ, to the twelve tribes dispersed abroad..." (Jam 1:1). James considered himself a slave of Christ. His belief in Christ not only attests to the resurrection but also to many other doctrines about Christ. It provides evidence for Christ's sinless life and the virgin birth. James would have known more about these things than anybody else, and yet, he still believed in Christ. He not only believed in Christ, but tradition says he died a martyr, stoned by the Jews around AD 62.[36]

The Case of the Apostle Paul

Another evidence that must be considered is that of the apostle Paul. Paul was a Pharisee and the son of a Pharisee (Acts 23:6). He was raised knowing Jewish law and the Greek and Hebrew languages. He studied under a renowned rabbi named Gamaliel (Acts 22:3 cf. Acts 5:34). As Christianity grew in popularity among the Jews, Paul zealously persecuted all who believed and taught it. He believed Christians were perverting the true way to salvation which came through the law, and not through faith in Jesus Christ. When Stephen attempted to preach the gospel to the Jews and was stoned for it, the Jews threw his clothes at Paul's feet (Acts 7:58, 8:1)—demonstrating his consent of their actions. Later, Paul received permission from the Jewish authorities to imprison anybody who professed Christ. However, while on his way to Damascus, Paul had a vision of the resurrected Christ which blinded him. Acts 9:3-5 describes this experience:

> As he was going along, approaching Damascus, suddenly a light from heaven flashed around him. He fell to the ground and heard a voice saying to him, "Saul, Saul, why are you persecuting me?" So he said, "Who are you, Lord?" He replied, "I am Jesus whom you are persecuting!

In addition, in 1 Corinthians 15:7-8, Paul shared this about seeing the resurrected Christ and his call to apostleship: "Then he appeared to James, then to all the apostles. Last of all, as though to one born at the wrong time, he appeared to me also." Paul considered himself "born at the wrong time" or "abnormally born" (NIV) because his call to apostleship happened after the resurrection, not before, like the original apostles.

Historians throughout the ages have been baffled at the historic figure of Paul—a Pharisee persecuting Christians, who professed to have seen the resurrected Christ, consequently converting, then becoming an apostle who preached to the Gentiles. He wrote almost half of the New Testament, was constantly persecuted for his faith, and died a martyr. It's like the historical figure of Hitler, who persecuted Jews, becoming a Jew and the greatest proponent of Judaism because he claimed to have seen a resurrected Moses. It sounds ridiculous! Yet, that is what Paul claimed about Christ, which has always baffled historians.

Consider how drastic Paul's change was: Not only did he profess Christ who he previously hated, but he also began to love Gentiles. Faithful Jews despised Gentiles. Jewish men commonly prayed a morning blessing thanking God they were Jews and not Gentile dogs, men and not women. But, after Paul's conversion, he was now the apostle to the Gentiles, spending his life on missionary journeys throughout Asia and Europe, seeking to reach them. In addition, Paul was considered the liberator of women. Most Jewish teachers would not teach women, and some wouldn't even look at them, to prevent lust; however, Paul championed the teaching of women and their dignity. In 1 Timothy 2:11, he says, "A woman must learn quietly with all submissiveness." This was radical during those days. Paul the persecutor of Christians, the racist, and misogynist now loved Jesus, Christians, Gentiles, and women!

Elias Andrews, a noted historian, said this:

> Many have found the radical transformation of this Pharisee of the Pharisees the most convincing evidence of the truth and power of religion to which he was converted, as well as the ultimate worth and place of the Person of Christ.[37]

In Paul's writings, he constantly spoke of his conversion and commitment to the resurrected Christ:

I have been crucified with Christ, and it is no longer I who live, but Christ lives in me. So the life I now live in the body, I live because of the faithfulness of the Son of God, who loved me and gave himself for me.
Galatians 2:20

But these assets I have come to regard as liabilities because of Christ. More than that, I now regard all things as liabilities compared to the far greater value of knowing Christ Jesus my Lord, for whom I have suffered the loss of all things—indeed, I regard them as dung!—that I may gain Christ
Philippians 3:7-8

But not only did Paul preach the resurrection, he also died for it. Tradition says he was decapitated in his second Roman imprisonment, around the mid-60s AD. His life is a tremendous evidence for the resurrection.

In fact, a story about two professors at Oxford who were initially antagonistic to Christianity shows the importance of Paul's conversion. As stated by Josh McDowell in his book, More than a Carpenter:

Two professors at Oxford, Gilbert West and Lord Lyttleton, were determined to destroy the basis of the Christian faith. West was going to demonstrate the fallacy of the resurrection and Lyttleton was going to prove that Saul of Tarsus had never converted to Christianity. Both men came to the opposite conclusion and became ardent followers of Jesus. Lord Lyttleton writes:

The conversion and apostleship of Saint Paul alone, duly considered, was of itself a demonstration sufficient to prove Christianity to be a Divine Revelation.

He concludes that if Paul's twenty-five years of suffering and service for Christ were a reality, then his conversion was true, for everything he did began with that sudden change. And if his conversion was true, Jesus Christ rose from the dead, for everything Paul was and did he attributed to the sight of the risen Christ.[38]

The Case of the Jews in Acts

Possibly, the strongest evidence for the resurrection is the conversion of many of the Jews who convinced Pilate to murder Christ. How is it possible that only weeks after Christ died, these Jews became followers of Christ? In Acts 2, Peter proclaimed the resurrection of the one they killed and called for their repentance and 3,000 of them were converted. Consider the following verses:

Men of Israel, listen to these words: Jesus the Nazarene, a man clearly attested to you by God with powerful deeds, wonders, and miraculous signs that God performed among you through him, just as you yourselves know—this man, who was handed over by the predetermined plan and foreknowledge of God, you executed by nailing him to a cross at the hands of Gentiles. But God raised him up, having released him from the pains of death, because it was not possible for him to be held in its power.
Acts 2:22-24

Therefore let all the house of Israel know beyond a doubt that God has made this Jesus whom you crucified both Lord and Christ." Now when they heard this, they were

acutely distressed and said to Peter and the rest of the apostles, "What should we do, brothers?" Peter said to them, "Repent, and each one of you be baptized in the name of Jesus Christ for the forgiveness of your sins, and you will receive the gift of the Holy Spirit.
Acts 2:36-38

So those who accepted his message were baptized, and that day about three thousand people were added. They were devoting themselves to the apostles' teaching and to fellowship, to the breaking of bread and to prayer.
Acts 2:41-42

Why were they converted? They had to be convinced that the resurrection was true. Not only did 3,000 convert, but in Acts 4:4, the number grew to 5,000. Historically, the early church boomed in Jerusalem, and then because of persecution, it spread throughout the ancient world and exists today as the biggest religion in the world.

How is this possible? It's baffling. (1) Some have tried to explain it away as a mass hallucination or dream. However, that makes no sense. How can thousands of people have the same hallucination? (2) Some have tried to explain it away as the development of a myth or legend. But again, that is illogical. Myths and legends can take generations to develop. They don't develop while the original audience is still alive and, certainly, not a few weeks after the event. Conclusions that deny a literal resurrection just don't make sense.

Again, the New Testament declares that after the resurrection, Christ appeared to the apostles and then 500 people over a period of forty days (1 Cor 15:6, Acts 1:3). These witnesses were throughout Jerusalem. The tomb was empty. The Roman soldiers, who typically would have been executed for failing to protect the tomb apparently were still alive (Matt 28:11-15), and the body of Christ was never found. The Jews who consented to Christ's death had to be totally convinced of his resurrection, because after publicly committing to Christ, they would have been persecuted for their newfound faith. Probably, contributing to their quick conversion was the fact that right after Christ's death, there was a major earthquake in Jerusalem and the bodies of other believers were resurrected (Matt 27:50-54). These Jews were convinced that Jesus was the Son of God and that he had resurrected.

Now it must be remembered, this isn't just something the Bible teaches. These are historical facts about the birth of the early church, well-attested by ancient Jewish and Roman historians. Jesus resurrected from the grave! No other conclusion makes sense.

Conclusion

How do we know Jesus is God? What are some evidences?

1. Evidence for Jesus' deity is *his teachings*. It is impossible to accept him as a good man, moral teacher, or prophet, which are the most common views of Jesus, while knowing the things he claimed, including being the Son of God. With the things he said and taught, he would either be a liar, lunatic, or demon.

2. Evidence for Jesus' deity is *the resurrection*. As mentioned, there is no ancient historical event more variously supported than the resurrection. If we reject the historical evidence for the resurrection, we must reject

much of what we know about ancient history, including the fact that Julius Caesar lived.

Next, we will consider more evidences for Jesus' deity—both in fulfilled prophecies and his miracles.

Reflection

1. What stood out most in the reading and why?
2. Why is it foolish to accept Jesus as a good man, wise teacher, or prophet from God when considering what he taught?
3. What are some historical evidences of Jesus' resurrection? Which historical evidence is the strongest to you and why?
4. What other questions and applications did you take from the reading?

Evidence for Christ's Deity: Prophecy and Miracles

What are further evidences that Jesus is God? Previously, we considered the illogical conclusions that many have about Christ—that he was simply a good man, moral teacher, or prophet from God. It is impossible to come to those conclusions when one considers what Jesus taught—he declared people's sins forgiven, claimed to be the only way to heaven, claimed to one day judge all of humanity, and to be the Son of God. As C.S. Lewis said, Jesus is either a liar, lunatic, the devil himself, or God as Jesus proclaimed.

We also looked at Jesus' resurrection as evidence for his deity. From a historical standpoint, there is no historical event better supported than the resurrection, including the fact that Julius Caesar even lived.[39]

What are some other evidences that help prove that Jesus is God? In this study, we will consider biblical prophecies and his miracles.

Prophecies about Jesus as Evidence of His Deity

As an illustration, let's say that we are going to the airport to pick up a person that we have never met or seen before, as a favor for a friend, named Susan. Susan said this person will be flying from Manila, Philippines to Seoul, Korea on Korean Air, Flight 257. That flight will land at 3:00 pm at Incheon Airport. Susan proceeds to give more information: "This person will meet you at baggage claim two. He has tan skin, brown eyes, and black hair. He is pretty short and average looking. He will be wearing grey sweats to be comfortable on his trip. The front of his hoody will say, 'Everything is more fun in the Philippines!' He was originally born in Manila but is moving to Korea to attend college. His social security number is xxxxxxx. His phone number is xxxxxxxx. His email is xxxxxx." We would think, "That's pretty thorough! We should be able to easily find this person!" Then, Susan adds that this person will stand on the baggage claim and yell, "I am Susan's friend! I am the one you are looking for! I'm from the Philippines. I'm here in Korea to go to college!" We would probably think, "Ok… this is a little much." Then Susan proceeds to give more information…

I share that exaggeration to say, the Bible is very much like that when giving details about the coming messiah. There are over 300 prophecies about Christ given in the Old Testament. All were given at least 400 years before he was born—some thousands of years before his birth. Thirty-three of these prophecies were fulfilled on the day of his crucifixion.[40]

When Christ made himself known to the Jews in the Gospels, consider what he said:

> You study the scriptures thoroughly because you think in them you possess eternal life, and it is these same scriptures that testify about me
> John 5:39

> If you believed Moses, you would believe me, because he wrote about me. But if you do not believe what Moses wrote, how will you believe my words?
> John 5:46-47

In fact, even after Christ resurrected, he pointed his disciples back to the Old Testament to encourage their faith in him. Luke 24:25-27 says,

> So he said to them, "You foolish people—how slow of heart to believe all that the prophets have spoken! Wasn't it necessary for the Christ to suffer these things and enter into his glory?" Then beginning with Moses and all the prophets, he interpreted to them the things written about himself in all the scriptures.

While Jesus was on the earth, he kept telling people to look at the Scriptures because they testified about him. In fact, after Jesus ascended, these OT prophecies were commonly used by the apostles to prove to the unbelieving Jews that Jesus was the messiah. Acts 17:2-3 says this about Paul's ministry in the synagogues:

> Paul went to the Jews in the synagogue, as he customarily did, and on three Sabbath days he addressed them from the scriptures, explaining and demonstrating that the Christ had to suffer and to rise from the dead, saying, "This Jesus I am proclaiming to you is the Christ."

What are these prophecies? Obviously, there are many, so we'll only consider a few:

The First Messianic Prophecy

> And I will put hostility between you and the woman and between your offspring and her offspring; her offspring will attack your head, and you will attack her offspring's heel." Genesis 3:15

84

In Genesis 3:15, the first gospel message is presented in Scripture. After Adam and Eve sinned against God, God pronounced the resulting curses and then promised that a male offspring would come from the woman to defeat the serpent, the devil. This serpent would strike the male offspring's heel—referring to a flesh wound—but the male would crush the serpent's head—referring to a fatal blow. On the cross, this cosmic battle happened. Christ's death on the cross pictured the male seed being bit. The pain was short-lived as Christ rose from the dead three days later. However, in Christ's death and resurrection, he dealt a death blow to Satan—he defeated him. Colossians 2:15 says, "Disarming the rulers and authorities, he has made a public disgrace of them, triumphing over them by the cross." Likewise, 1 John 3:8 says, "...For this purpose the Son of God was revealed: to destroy the works of the devil." The full outworking of this defeat won't take place until the end times when Christ throws Satan into the lake of fire to be tormented forever (Rev 20:10). In addition, Christ will remove the curse from the creation and renew the heavens and the earth—making them a new heaven and earth (Rev 21). There will be no evil, sorrow, or death there. The first prophecy was given right after the first sin. A male seed would come to undo the evil and chaos Satan had brought by tempting Adam and Eve to sin.

Prophecy of the Virgin Birth

In Isaiah 7:14 (NIV), further revelation is given about the messiah. He would be born of a virgin. It says, "Therefore the Lord himself will give you a sign: The virgin will conceive and give birth to a son, and will call him Immanuel."

Though this prophecy has some type of dual fulfillment with Isaiah's wife having a child as a sign to Israel (Is 8:11-4, 18), it is ultimately fulfilled in the Gospels with Christ's birth. Luke 1:34-

35 tells the story, as Mary responds to a prophecy about this from an angel:

> Mary said to the angel, "How will this be, since I have not had sexual relations with a man?" The angel replied, "The Holy Spirit will come upon you, and the power of the Most High will overshadow you. Therefore the child to be born will be holy; he will be called the Son of God.

Matthew directly applies this event to Isaiah 7:14:

> This all happened so that what was spoken by the Lord through the prophet would be fulfilled: "Look! The virgin will conceive and bear a son, and they will call him Emmanuel," which means "God with us."
> Matthew 1:22-23

Evidence for the Virgin Birth

Are there any evidences for the virgin birth? Obviously, we see evidences in how Christ's followers (Matthew and Luke) perceived his birth, as they wrote about it in the Gospels. But, we also see something in the Gospels about how those who rejected Christ perceived his birth. In Mark 6:3, consider how the Jews from Christ's hometown responded to him: "'Isn't this the carpenter, the son of Mary and brother of James, Joses, Judas, and Simon? And aren't his sisters here with us?' And so they took offense at him."

What should stand out is how they called him "the son of Mary." This was probably an insult in that culture. Jews were called by the name of their father or grandfather, even when they were dead (cf. Lk 4:22, John 6:42).[41] For example, they would be called the "son of Abraham" or the "son of David." They were only called by the son of a woman when that child's paternity was doubted—

when they didn't know who the father was. Though this does not confirm the virgin birth; it does confirm that it was well-known that Joseph was not the baby's father and that nobody knew who Jesus' father was. Christ's birth was perceived to have happened by fornication—sex outside of marriage.

We may see further evidence for this in how the Pharisees responded to Jesus. In John 8:41, when Christ was speaking to the Pharisees, he told them they did the deeds of their father the devil and they responded back, "We were not born of fornication; we have one Father—God." When they said, "We were not born of fornication," this was probably a jab at the paternity of Christ (cf. John 8:19).[42] They were essentially saying, "We are not unholy, but you probably are because nobody knows who your father is."

When considering the virgin birth, we have the witness of Christ's followers, through the Holy Spirit, but we also have the witness of how those who rejected him perceived his birth. Apparently, nobody knew who Christ's father was.

Why did God choose for the messiah to be born of a virgin?

1. The virgin birth was necessary for the uniting of the Divine and human natures. Christ had to be human to die for humanity, and he had to be God to pay for the sins of the entire world. Christ's humanity came through his mother, and his deity came through the work of the Holy Spirit in her womb. Hebrews 2:14 says,

> Therefore, since the children share in flesh and blood, he likewise shared in their humanity, so that through death he could destroy the one who holds the power of death (that is, the devil),

2. The virgin birth is also a reminder that salvation must come through God. Salvation could never come through human

effort. It had to be a Divine miracle, as God intervened to save people condemned to hell. Galatians 4:4-5 says, "But when the appropriate time had come, God sent out his Son, born of a woman, born under the law, to redeem those who were under the law, so that we may be adopted as sons with full rights."

Prophecy of Being Abraham's Seed

What are some other prophecies about Christ? Not only was the messiah to be born of a virgin, he was going to be born in Abraham's lineage. In Genesis 22:18 (NIV), God said this to Abraham, "and through your offspring all nations on earth will be blessed, because you have obeyed me" (cf. Gal 3:16). Later, it was confirmed that the seed would not only come through Abraham, but his son, Isaac; Isaac's son, Jacob; then Jacob's son, Judah.

Prophecy of His Kingship

In a prophecy about the messiah coming through Judah, more details about this child are gained. Genesis 49:10 says, "The scepter will not depart from Judah, nor the ruler's staff from between his feet, until he comes to whom it belongs; the nations will obey him." All the nations will submit to this prophesied male seed.

This prophecy is further clarified in God's words to David. David was Israel's second king, and he came from the tribe of Judah. God said this to David in 1 Chronicles 17:11-14 (ESV):

> When your days are fulfilled to walk with your fathers, I will raise up your offspring after you, one of your own sons, and I will establish his kingdom. He shall build a house for me, and I will establish his throne forever. I will be to him a

father, and he shall be to me a son. I will not take my steadfast love from him, as I took it from him who was before you, but I will confirm him in my house and in my kingdom forever, and his throne shall be established forever.

Like many other prophecies, this one has a partial fulfillment and a secondary fulfillment. It is partially fulfilled in Solomon who builds God a temple. But Solomon could never fully fulfill this prophecy, as it promises a seed with an everlasting rule. Further prophecies clarify a future, eternal Davidic reign. Jeremiah 23:5 says:

I, the LORD, promise that a new time will certainly come when I will raise up for them a righteous branch, a descendant of David. He will rule over them with wisdom and understanding and will do what is just and right in the land.

Jeremiah prophesied many years after David and Solomon had died. There would be a future, eternal Davidic king.

God answered this prophecy in Jesus. Mary and Joseph were distant cousins who were both in David's lineage. In Matthew 1, Joseph's genealogy is presented. Since Jesus was adopted by Joseph, he was in the legal line of David, which was always established through the father.[43] In Luke 3:23-37, Mary's genealogy is presented, which established Jesus as in the bloodline of David. Since Jews did not normally include women in their genealogies, Luke actually places Joseph in the genealogy instead of Mary. Luke 3:23 says, "So Jesus, when he began his ministry, was about thirty years old. He was the son (as was supposed) of Joseph, the son of Heli." Two evidences that the Luke 3 genealogy is not really Joseph's line (1) is the fact that it differs from Matthew's. (2) Also, in the phrase "Joseph, the son of Heli" (Lk 3:23), the "of" before Heli is the only one in the genealogy that is not genitive (possessive).[44] Heli was not Joseph's genetic father—he was Mary's. Therefore, most scholars believe Luke gives Mary's genealogy.

Why did both parents come through the line of David? God was making it clear. This child is the prophesied messiah! He is the promised seed of David. In fact, throughout the Gospels, people recognized Jesus as the prophesied Son of David and called him by that prophetic title (Lk 18:38, Mk 10:47). In Matthew 21:9, as Israel recognized him as the messiah when he entered Jerusalem, they shouted, "Hosanna to the Son of David! Blessed is the one who comes in the name of the Lord! Hosanna in the highest!" Hosanna means, "Please, save us!"[45] They were waiting for Christ, the messiah, to save them.

Future Messiah?

Is it possible that the Gospels messed up and that there could be a future messiah, like many orthodox Jews believe? As we consider genealogies, it is good to remember that these were kept at the Jewish temple, and in AD 70, when the Romans destroyed Jerusalem and the Jewish temple, the genealogical records were destroyed.[46] Therefore, to have an actual genealogical record of Davidic lineage (and not just word of mouth), the messiah had to have come before AD 70.

This leaves only one complete lineage left that can be used to prove that a future person is the messiah and that is Jesus'. He came through Abraham, Isaac, Jacob, Judah, and David. He was the son of David, born of a virgin, as Scripture prophesied. This is true of Jesus and only Jesus. Jesus is the messiah!

Prophecy of the Time Frame of Christ

In Daniel 9:25, we see a startling prophecy giving the actual timeframe that the messiah would be on the earth. The background is Daniel praying about the future of Israel (Dan 9:1-3) when the angel, Gabriel, appears and shares with him about Israel's future, including the coming of the messiah. Consider verse 25:

> From the issuing of the command to restore and rebuild Jerusalem until an anointed one, a prince arrives, there will be a period of seven weeks and sixty-two weeks. It will again be built, with plaza and moat, but in distressful times.

When the angel referred to "weeks," it could also be translated "sevens," as in the NIV. This could mean seven days or years.[47] Years makes the most sense, because the context deals with Israel's long-term future including the coming of the messiah and also because Daniel had already been thinking in terms of years (Israel's seventy years of exile, Daniel 9:2). The angel Gabriel said to Daniel, it would be seven sevens (49) plus sixty-two sevens (434) until the messiah comes. Altogether that equals 483 years (49 +434= 483). From the issuing of the decree to rebuild Jerusalem until the messiah came would be 483 years. Gabriel adds that Jerusalem would be rebuilt in "distressful times." The book of Nehemiah tells us that while Nehemiah led Israel in rebuilding Jerusalem's walls, there was much persecution. In one scene, the Israelites did their work with one hand and held a weapon in the other (Neh 4:17).

Though Israel was sent back to their land by Cyrus, the issuing of the decree to rebuild Israel was given by King Artaxerxes to Nehemiah in 444 B.C (Neh 2).[48] When one takes into account that the Jewish calendar was 360 days and not 365 as ours is

91

today, 483 years later would be 33 AD—right around the time of Christ's death.[49]

Those who have actually counted the days say that the prophecy was fulfilled on Palm Sunday[50]—the day when Jesus rode into the streets of Jerusalem on a donkey, and the people shouted, "Hosanna! Hosanna!" as they recognized Jesus as the messiah. Consider what Jesus said about the city on that very day:

> Now when Jesus approached and saw the city, he wept over it, saying, "If you had only known on this day, even you, the things that make for peace! But now they are hidden from your eyes. For the days will come upon you when your enemies will build an embankment against you and surround you and close in on you from every side. They will demolish you—you and your children within your walls—and they will not leave within you one stone on top of another, because you did not recognize the time of your visitation from God."
> Luke 19:41-44

Daniel 9:25 prophesies the exact day Christ would be on the earth, so Israel would be ready to accept their messiah. However, they failed to give attention to the prophecy and instead crucified the Son of God—bringing judgment upon themselves.

What are some of the other prophecies which give evidence that Jesus is the messiah, the son of God?

Prophecy of Christ's Birthplace

Micah predicted over 700 years before Christ's birth that Jesus would be born in Bethlehem.[51] There were two Bethlehem's in Israel, and Micah even predicts the one in Judah. Micah 5:2 says, "As for you, Bethlehem Ephrathah, seemingly insignificant among the clans of Judah—from you a king will emerge who will rule over Israel on my behalf, one whose origins are in the distant past." Matthew 2:1-2, 5-6 gives the fulfillment:

> After Jesus was born in Bethlehem in Judea, in the time of King Herod, wise men from the East came to Jerusalem saying, "Where is the one who is born king of the Jews? For we saw his star when it rose and have come to worship him." ... "In Bethlehem of Judea," they said, "for it is written this way by the prophet: 'And you, Bethlehem, in the land of Judah, are in no way least among the rulers of Judah, for out of you will come a ruler who will shepherd my people Israel.'"

Thirty-three Prophecies on the Day of Christ's Death

As mentioned, thirty-three prophecies were fulfilled on the day of Christ's death. Let's consider a few:

- He would be betrayed by a friend (Ps 41:9).
- The price of the betrayal would be thirty pieces of silver (Zech 11:12).
- The money would be used to buy a potter's field (Zech 11:13).
- He would be forsaken and deserted by his disciples (Zech 13:7).
- He would be accused by false witnesses (Psalm 35:11).
- He would be silent before his witnesses (Isaiah 53:7).
- He would be wounded and bruised (Isaiah 53:5).
- He would be hated without cause (Psalm 69:4).
- He would be struck and spit on (Isaiah 50:6).
- He would be mocked, ridiculed, and rejected (Isaiah 53:3).

- He would collapse in weakness (Psalm 109:24-25).
- He would be taunted with specific words (Psalm 22:6-8).
- People would shake their heads at him (Psalm 109:25).
- He would be executed among sinners (Isaiah 53:12).
- His hands and feet would be pierced (Psalm 22:16).
- He would pray for his persecutors (Isaiah 53:12).
- His friends and family would stand afar off (Psalm 38:11).
- His garments would be divided and won by casting lots (Psalm 22:18).
- He would be given gall and vinegar (Psalm 69:21).
- His bones would be left unbroken (Psalm 34:20).
- He would die for our sins (Isaiah 53: 4–6).
- His side would be pierced (Zech 12:10).
- He would be buried in a rich man's tomb (Isaiah 53:9).

Prophecy of Christ's Resurrection

In Psalm 16:10 (NIV), David prophesied Christ's resurrection when he said, "because you will not abandon me to the realm of the dead, nor will you let your faithful one see decay." In considering David's writing, Peter said it was fulfilled in Jesus: "David by foreseeing this spoke about the resurrection of the Christ, that he was neither abandoned to Hades, nor did his body experience decay. This Jesus God raised up, and we are all witnesses of it" (Acts 2:31-32). Isaiah seemingly prophesied it as well:

> Yet it was the LORD's will to crush him and cause him to suffer, and though the LORD makes his life an offering for sin, he will see his offspring and prolong his days, and the will of the LORD will prosper in his hand
> Isaiah 53:10 (NIV)

Now as we consider all these prophecies, certainly we must declare, "This is pretty convincing! If Jesus fulfilled all those prophecies, he must be the Son of God—he must be the seed that everybody was waiting for!"

What is the probability that a person would fulfill only eight of the Old Testament prophecies about Christ? Professor Peter W. Stoner states that the probability of just eight prophecies being fulfilled in one person is 1×10^{17th}. That is 100,000,000,000,000,000.

It has been illustrated like this: If you took 1×10^{17} silver dollars and placed them over Texas (the second largest US state), you would not only cover all of Texas but would have a coin pile two feet deep. If you blindfolded yourself, took one of the coins and threw it back into the pile, and walked from the beginning of Texas, stopping only once to find that coin, that is the chance that one person would fulfill only eight of these prophecies.[52]

The prophetic evidence concerning Christ is simply amazing! Again, the Old Testament gives over 300 prophecies that were fulfilled in Christ's first coming and thirty-three which were fulfilled on the day of Christ's death. Each of these prophecies was written at least 400 years before Christ's birth—some of them thousands of years before his birth. God went to extraordinary lengths to make sure that the prophesied messiah was unmistakable to those who were genuinely looking. In addition, we must consider that all these fulfilled prophecies about Christ's first coming should give us great confidence in the prophetic accuracy of the second coming.

Jesus' Own Prophecies as Evidence of His Deity

What about Jesus' own prophecies? We've covered OT prophecies about him to help prove his deity, but what about prophecies he gave? Were they accurate? We'll consider a few:

The Resurrection

In John 2:19, Jesus said, "Destroy this temple and in three days I will raise it up again." As mentioned, there is no other ancient event or person more supported by historical evidence. We have more evidence for Christ's resurrection than that Julius Caesar even lived.

Destruction of the Temple

In Matthew 24:2, Jesus said this about the temple, "Do you see all these things? I tell you the truth, not one stone will be left on another. All will be torn down!" In AD 70, the Romans destroyed the temple, almost forty years after Christ's death.

Persecution of Believers

Jesus predicted that his disciples would receive great persecution after his death and especially towards the end times. In Matthew 24:9, Christ said, "Then they will hand you over to be persecuted and will kill you. You will be hated by all the nations because of my name." That certainly happened to the apostles and the early church. The early church expanded from Jerusalem throughout the ancient world primarily because of persecution. Today, as Christ prophesied, persecution has grown. In fact, in the twentieth century, there were more martyrs for Christ than in the rest of the centuries combined. Some have estimated that around 90,000 Christians are martyred yearly—which would mean 246 per day.[53]

Antichrists

Finally, Christ also predicted that there would be many false Christs and false prophets in the last days. Consider the following verses:

> Jesus answered them, "Watch out that no one misleads you. For many will come in my name, saying, 'I am the Christ,' and they will mislead many.
> Matthew 24:4-5

> Then if anyone says to you, 'Look, here is the Christ!' or 'There he is!' do not believe him. For false messiahs and false prophets will appear and perform great signs and wonders to deceive, if possible, even the elect. Remember, I have told you ahead of time.
> Matthew 24:23-25

In Korea alone, there have been around 120 self-proclaimed messiahs, with about seventy having large followings.[54] In addition to the many false messiahs which Christ predicted, there are many false prophets in Christianity as well. Essentially, there are new Christian cults almost every day—teaching doctrines that conflict with the fundamentals of the Christian faith. All these things Christ predicted, which gives credence to his claim of deity.

Jesus' Miracles as Evidence of His Deity

The final evidence we will consider which points to Jesus being God is his miracles. In fact, Jesus often challenged people to consider his miracles as evidence for his identity. Consider Christ's response to John's disciples in Matthew 11:2-5:

Now when John heard in prison about the deeds Christ had done, he sent his disciples to ask a question: "Are you the one who is to come, or should we look for another?" Jesus answered them, "Go tell John what you hear and see: The blind see, the lame walk, lepers are cleansed, the deaf hear, the dead are raised, and the poor have good news proclaimed to them.

Why did Jesus point John to his miracles? In the Old Testament, these works were prophesied of the messiah. Isaiah 35:4-6 says:

Tell those who panic, "Be strong! Do not fear! Look, your God comes to avenge! With divine retribution he comes to deliver you." Then blind eyes will open, deaf ears will hear. Then the lame will leap like a deer, the mute tongue will shout for joy; for water will flow in the desert, streams in the wilderness.

Of course, Christ did not only open the eyes of the blind, heal the lame and mute, he also calmed the storms, turned water into wine, multiplied fish and bread to feed multitudes, and raised the dead, among other things. Again, Christ constantly pointed to these as evidence. Consider the following verses:

Jesus replied, "I told you and you do not believe. The deeds I do in my Father's name testify about me.
John 10:25

But if I do them, even if you do not believe me, believe the deeds, so that you may come to know and understand that I am in the Father and the Father is in me."

John 10:38

Historical Evidence for Miracles

Well then, one must ask, "Is there any historical evidence for these miracles?" Yes, there is. For example, in the Jewish Babylonian Talmud, which is a collection of Jewish Rabbinical writings, it says:

> On the eve of Passover Yeshu was hanged. For forty days before the execution took place, a herald went forth and cried, "He is going forth to be stoned because he has practiced sorcery and enticed Israel to apostasy.[55]

Since the Jews rejected Jesus as the messiah, they called his works "sorcery." In addition, Josephus, an ancient Jewish Historian who was not a follower of Christ, called Jesus, "a worker of amazing deeds."[56]

Christ declared that miracles proved his Divine nature, and these miracles are well attested by historical evidence—evidence written by his followers (such as Matthew, Mark, Luke, and John) and by those who rejected his claim to be the prophesied messiah.

Conclusion

How do we know Jesus is God?

1. Evidence for Jesus' deity is *his teachings*. It is impossible to accept him as a good man, moral teacher, or prophet, which are the most common views of Jesus, while knowing the things he claimed, including being the Son of God. With the things he said and taught, if he is not God, then he would either be a liar, lunatic, or demon.

2. Evidence for Jesus' deity is *the resurrection*. As mentioned, there is no ancient historical event more variously supported than the resurrection. If we reject the historical evidence for the resurrection, we must reject much of what we know about ancient history.

3. Evidence for Jesus' deity is *fulfilled prophecy*. Christ fulfilled over 300 OT prophecies, including thirty-three on the day of his crucifixion. If fulfilling prophecies were not enough, we have the accuracy of his own prophecies, including his own death and resurrection, the destruction of the temple, the appearance of false messiah's claiming to be him, among other things, which testify to his deity.

4. Evidence for Jesus' deity is *the miracles he performed*. Christ continually pointed people to his working of miracles to confirm his identity. He healed the lame and the blind, resurrected people from the dead, and calmed the storms and the sea, among other things. There is strong historical evidence of these from both his followers (the authors of the Gospels) and those who rejected him (Jewish teachers and historians).

Do all these evidences prove that Jesus is God? If not, it certainly gives strong evidence for the belief. Jesus Christ is God, and one day all will call him, Lord, and bow to him (Phil 2:9-11). However, for some, their declaration of faith in Christ being Lord will be too late to save them (cf. John 3:16). Will you believe in Christ and follow him?

Reflection

1. What stood out most in the reading and why?
2. How does fulfilled Bible prophecies (those about Christ and those he gave) provide evidence for Christ's deity and also the validity of Scripture?
3. Why is the virgin birth important?
4. Roughly, how many Old Testament prophecies were fulfilled in Christ's first coming?
5. How many Old Testament prophecies were fulfilled in Christ on the day of his crucifixion?
6. What are some prophecies that Christ gave which have already been fulfilled?
7. What other questions or applications did you take from the reading?

Typology of Christ

Not only does the Old Testament reveal the coming messiah through prophecy, it also reveals him through typology. Typology refers to historical people, places, objects, or events which foreshadow Christ and his work in the Old Testament. Consider the verses below, which speak of OT typology:

> Therefore do not let anyone judge you with respect to food or drink, or in the matter of a feast, new moon, or Sabbath days—these are only the shadow of the things to come, but the reality is Christ!
> Colossians 2:16-17

> For the law possesses a shadow of the good things to come but not the reality itself, and is therefore completely unable, by the same sacrifices offered continually, year after year, to perfect those who come to worship.
> Hebrews 10:1

Many of the laws, festivals, and stories in the Old Testament were simply shadows of the coming messiah—meant to prepare Israel for him. As with shadows today, they reflect aspects of something real but do not fully give the picture. In this study, we will consider many of the Old Testament types of Christ.

Adam

Adam is a type of Christ. Adam was the leader of the world who failed when tempted by the devil, leading the world into sin and death. However, Christ, like Adam, was tempted by the devil but succeeded and leads his followers to righteousness and eternal life. Adam was simply an imperfect shadow of a coming perfect, human ruler. Consider the following verses:

> So also it is written, "The first man, Adam, became a living person"; the last Adam became a life-giving spirit.
> 1 Corinthians 15:45

> For since death came through a man, the resurrection of the dead also came through a man. For just as in Adam all die, so also in Christ all will be made alive.
> 1 Corinthians 15:21-22

> Yet death reigned from Adam until Moses even over those who did not sin in the same way that Adam (who is a type of the coming one) transgressed... For if, by the transgression of the one man, death reigned through the one, how much more will those who receive the abundance of grace and of the gift of righteousness reign in life through the one, Jesus Christ!
> Romans 5:14, 17

Tony Evans said this in comparing Adam and Christ—the last Adam (1 Cor 15:21-22):

> ...the first Adam was a death-dealer, the last Adam is a life-giver. People who are related only to the first Adam will only see physical life. Their future is eternal death. But

people who are related to the last Adam not only have the life of the first Adam physically, they have the life of the last Adam eternally, which is a better life.[57]

Abel

Abel is a type of Christ. Abel, the son of Adam, was murdered by his older brother, Cain, simply for being righteous. Likewise, Christ was murdered by his brethren, the Jews, for being righteous. When God approached Cain about the murder in Genesis 4:10-11, God said:

> But the LORD said, "What have you done? The voice of your brother's blood is crying out to me from the ground! So now, you are banished from the ground, which has opened its mouth to receive your brother's blood from your hand.

Abel's blood spoke about the need for justice. In contrast, Christ's blood speaks about the need for mercy, forgiveness, and salvation. Hebrews 12:24 says, "and to Jesus, the mediator of a new covenant, and to the sprinkled blood that speaks of something better than Abel's does." Also, Ephesians 1:7 says, "In him we have redemption through his blood, the forgiveness of our trespasses, according to the riches of his grace."

Noah's Ark

Also, Noah's ark is a type of Christ. In the same way that God saved Noah's family who entered the ark from the judgment of the flood, God now saves all who are in Christ. All outside of Christ will experience God's eternal wrath. First Peter 3:20-21 says:

after they were disobedient long ago when God patiently waited in the days of Noah as an ark was being constructed. In the ark a few, that is eight souls, were delivered through water. And this prefigured baptism, which now saves you—not the washing off of physical dirt but the pledge of a good conscience to God—through the resurrection of Jesus Christ,

When verse 21 says this "prefigured baptism," the word "prefigured" can also be translated "type" or "antitype." The ark which saved Noah's family from God's judgment through water prefigures a future baptism. Peter makes it clear that he is not referring to "water baptism," as he says, "not the washing off of physical dirt" but the "pledge of a good conscience to God— through the resurrection of Jesus Christ" (v. 21). Those who put their faith in Christ are baptized into him, including his death and resurrection, and they will be saved from God's future wrath. Several verses point to this spiritual baptism into Christ:

For just as the body is one and yet has many members, and all the members of the body—though many—are one body, so too is Christ. For in one Spirit we were all baptized into one body. Whether Jews or Greeks or slaves or free, we were all made to drink of the one Spirit.
1 Corinthians 12:12-13

Or do you not know that as many as were baptized into Christ Jesus were baptized into his death? Therefore we have been buried with him through baptism into death, in order that just as Christ was raised from the dead through the glory of the Father, so we too may live a new life. For if we have become united with him in the likeness of his

death, we will certainly also be united in the likeness of his resurrection.
Romans 6:3-5

Baptism really means to be "identified" with something. Those who by faith accept Christ as Lord and Savior are identified with his life, death, and resurrection and, therefore, will be saved from God's judgment. Noah's ark was a type of Christ, in that people who identify with him will likewise be saved.

Melchizedek

Melchizedek was a king of Salem (an old name for Jerusalem) and priest of Yahweh who met with Abraham in Genesis 14. Abraham honored Melchizedek by paying tithes to him (v. 20). One of the things that makes Melchizedek unique is that he was a king and priest. In Israel, those roles were kept distinct. The king was not a priest, and the priest was not a king. Kings were supposed to come from the line of David and priests from the Levitical line, through Aaron's children.

In Hebrews 7, the author makes the argument that the New Covenant is greater than the Old Covenant because it has a greater priesthood. God promised that Christ would be a priest like Melchizedek instead of a Levitical priest. The priesthood of Melchizedek is greater than the Levitical priesthood for at least two reasons: As mentioned, Abraham, who is the grandfather of Levi, paid tithes to Melchizedek which shows how great Melchizedek was (Heb 4:9). Also, because there is no record of Melchizedek's death, that means he has an eternal priesthood. Hebrews 7:3 says this about him, "Without father, without mother, without genealogy, he has neither beginning of days nor end of life but is like the son of God, and he remains a priest for all time." Priests typically remained in office till death (Heb 7:23). Therefore, since there is no record of Melchizedek's death, technically, he remains a priest. Because of this, Melchizedek is a type of Christ—a priest and king, with an eternal priesthood.

Jacob's Ladder

Another type of Christ is Jacob's ladder. In Genesis 28, Jacob has a vision of a heavenly ladder with angels ascending to heaven on it and descending to earth from it (v. 12). In John 1:50-51, when Christ met with Nathaniel—who became one of the original twelve disciples—he said this to him:

> ... "Because I told you that I saw you under the fig tree, do you believe? You will see greater things than these." He continued, "I tell all of you the solemn truth—you will see heaven opened and the angels of God ascending and descending on the Son of Man."

Nathaniel, as one raised hearing and studying the Old Testament stories, would have quickly understood the picture Christ gave. Jacob's ladder typified Christ, and therefore, Christ was the way to heaven. Likewise, in John 14:6, Jesus said, "I am the way, and the truth, and the life. No one comes to the Father except through me."

Isaac

Though Isaac is never clearly called a type of Christ in Scripture, many have seen the similarities as unmistakable. Isaac was the child God promised to give Abraham. Isaac had a miraculous birth when Abraham was 100 years old and Abraham's wife, Sara, was 90 years old. Abraham was called by God to sacrifice Isaac; however, Isaac was miraculously delivered from

Abraham's knife as God provided a ram in a thicket. The reason Abraham was willing to sacrifice Isaac was because he believed God would raise him from the dead. Hebrews 11:17-19 says this:

> By faith Abraham, when he was tested, offered up Isaac. He had received the promises, yet he was ready to offer up his only son. God had told him, "Through Isaac descendants will carry on your name," and he reasoned that God could even raise him from the dead, and in a sense he received him back from there.

Likewise, Christ was the only begotten Son of God. He was prophesied about soon after the creation of the earth. He had a miraculous birth, as he was born of a virgin. God chose to sacrifice him, as a substitutionary lamb, for the sins of the world and then raised him from the dead. Though never clearly declared a type of Christ, the similarities between Isaac and Christ are unmistakable.

Joseph

Likewise, Joseph is never clearly called a type of Christ, but the similarities are many. Joseph was the favorite child of his father, Jacob. He was hated by his brothers and sold into slavery in Egypt. While a slave, he was eventually falsely accused by his master's wife and thrown into prison. While there, he interpreted Pharaoh's dream of seven years of plenty in the land and seven years of famine. Because of that, Pharaoh promoted him to second in command of Egypt in order to prepare the country to survive the famine. Eventually, as second in command, Joseph also saves his family, including the brothers who enslaved him, and other nations from starving during the famine. God used the bad that happened to him to save many lives.

What are some of the ways people have seen unmistakable similarities with Christ? Here are a few:

- He was a seed of Abraham whom the nations of the earth were blessed through, even as Christ was (Gen 41:53-57; cf. Gen 22:18).
- He was the beloved son of his father, even as Christ was (John 3:16).
- He became a poor servant, even as Christ did (2 Cor 8:9).
- His brothers hated him because of his dream that one day he would reign over them (37:4,8). The Jews hated Christ and would not have him reign over them (Lk 19:14).
- The Jewish brothers would eventually bow down to Joseph, even though they previously rejected and harmed him. Likewise, Israel initially rejected Christ and killed him, but one day they will submit to him and worship him as their messiah (Zech 12:10, Rom 11:26-27).
- Joseph and Jesus were betrayed by their brothers (the Jews) and sold for the price of a slave in pieces of silver (Gen 37:28, Matt 26:15).
- Joseph was exalted to prince in Egypt. Everything was under Joseph's rule except Pharaoh. In Genesis 41:40, Pharaoh said, " Only I, the king, will be greater than you." Likewise, God has exalted Christ. First Corinthians 15:27 says, "For he has put everything in subjection under his feet. But when it says 'everything' has been put in subjection, it is clear that this does not include the one who put everything in subjection to him."
- Joseph was given a Gentile wife, an Egyptian. Christ has been given a bride who is both Jew and Gentile, the church (Eph 2:11-22, 5:25-26, Gal 3:28, Rev 19:7-8).
- Joseph wept over his brothers (Gen 45:2). Christ wept over the sins of the Jews as well (Lk 19:41).

- Joseph was a prophet that received messages from God. Jesus was "the Prophet" (Deut 18:15, John 7:40, Acts 3:18-22).
- Joseph saved the lives of those who came to him for help, including many nations in the world (Gen 41:57). Likewise, Christ saves the lives of those who come to him for help (John 3:16).

Again, though never clearly pointed to in Scripture as a type of Christ, Joseph's story, in many ways, mirrors that of Jesus.

Moses

Moses is also a type of Christ. As God made Moses the mediator of the Old Covenant, Christ is the mediator of the New Covenant. Moses even prophesied that there would be a prophet like him who would come that Israel must listen to. Deuteronomy 18:15-19 says:

> The LORD your God will raise up for you a prophet like me from among you—from your fellow Israelites; you must listen to him. This accords with what happened at Horeb in the day of the assembly. You asked the LORD your God: "Please do not make us hear the voice of the LORD our God any more or see this great fire any more lest we die." The LORD then said to me, "What they have said is good. I will raise up a prophet like you for them from among their fellow Israelites. I will put my words in his mouth and he will speak to them whatever I command. I will personally hold responsible anyone who then pays no attention to the words that prophet speaks in my name.

Since "the Prophet" became a messianic title, the Jews were waiting for him and recognized Christ as that prophet. Consider the following verses:

> Now when the people saw the miraculous sign that Jesus performed, they began to say to one another, "This is certainly the Prophet who is to come into the world."
> John 6:14

> When they heard these words, some of the crowd began to say, "This really is the Prophet!"
> John 7:40

Passover Lamb

The Jewish Passover lamb is also a type of Christ. While Israel was in Egypt, God judged the Egyptians by killing their firstborns. The Jews were passed over as long as they had the blood of a lamb sprinkled on their doorposts (Ex 12:3-14). During the Passover ceremony, they would not eat yeast, but would cleanse their house of it, which was a picture of getting rid of sin. Likewise, Paul said that Christ is our Passover lamb who has been slain to deliver us from God's judgment. Therefore, we should also get rid of yeast in our lives and churches—referring to sin. First Corinthians 5:7 says: "Clean out the old yeast so that you may be a new batch of dough—you are, in fact, without yeast. For Christ, our Passover lamb, has been sacrificed."

Manna

God sending manna from heaven to sustain Israel in the wilderness is also a type of Christ. In Exodus 16, the Israelites complained to God because they lacked food while traveling in the wilderness. So God gave them manna from heaven to eat, which was a type of bread. Likewise, while Christ was speaking to the Jews about their need to believe in him, they asked for a sign from God, just like their fathers received manna from God in the wilderness. Christ simply responded that he was the bread from heaven—declaring that God sending manna from heaven to satisfy his people in the wilderness was always a picture of him. In the same way God gave the Israelites bread to deliver them from hunger and preserve their lives, God gave Christ, as bread from heaven, to satisfy and save all who believe in him. John 6:30-35 says:

> So they said to him, "Then what miraculous sign will you perform, so that we may see it and believe you? What will you do? Our ancestors ate the manna in the wilderness, just as it is written, 'He gave them bread from heaven to eat.'" Then Jesus told them, "I tell you the solemn truth, it is not Moses who has given you the bread from heaven, but my Father is giving you the true bread from heaven. For the bread of God is the one who comes down from heaven and gives life to the world." So they said to him, "Sir, give us this bread all the time!" Jesus said to them, "I am the bread of life. The one who comes to me will never go hungry, and the one who believes in me will never be thirsty.

The Bronze Snake

The bronze snake that Moses erected for Israel to save them from death is a type of Christ. In Numbers 21, while in the wilderness, the Israelites complained and murmured against God. Because of their complaining, God disciplined them by allowing them to be bit by poisonous snakes. Then, when Moses prayed for them, God told Moses to raise a bronze snake on a pole, and when the Israelites looked at the snake, they would be healed. In John 3:14-15, Christ compared himself to the bronze snake. He said, "Just as Moses lifted up the serpent in the wilderness, so must the Son of Man be lifted up, so that everyone who believes in him may have eternal life." The bronze snake was always a picture of Christ. In the world, people are dying from the deadly poison of sin; however, when they put their faith in Christ who died on the cross for their sins, they will be saved.

High Priest

The high priest in the Old Covenant is also a type of Christ. In the Old Covenant, God established priests to mediate between the people and God. They would pray for the people, offer sacrifices for them, and minister to God on their behalf. Among the priests, there was a high priest, who once a year would go into the inner sanctuary of the temple to offer an atoning sacrifice for sins. Scripture says that Christ is our high priest—our mediator between us and God. However, unlike regular high priests, he is a perfect priest in that he has never sinned, and he will live forever. Consider the below verses:

> For we do not have a high priest incapable of sympathizing with our weaknesses, but one who has been tempted in every way just as we are, yet without sin. Therefore let us confidently approach the throne of grace to receive mercy and find grace whenever we need help.
> Hebrews 4:15-16

> For it is indeed fitting for us to have such a high priest: holy, innocent, undefiled, separate from sinners, and exalted above the heavens. He has no need to do every day what

those priests do, to offer sacrifices first for their own sins and then for the sins of the people, since he did this in offering himself once for all.
Hebrews 7:26-27

Tabernacle

The tabernacle is a type of Christ. While Moses was leading Israel in the wilderness, God had them make a tabernacle, which was a portable tent, where God would come down to meet with his people. John the apostle called Christ our tabernacle. In John 1:14, he says, "Now the Word became flesh and took up residence among us. We saw his glory—the glory of the one and only, full of grace and truth, who came from the Father." The phrase "took up residence" or "dwelt" (ESV) in the Greek actually means "tabernacled."[58] Where God's presence came down to the tabernacle to meet with Israel in the Old Testament, in Christ, God came down to meet with his people.

The Sacrificial Lamb

Sacrificial lambs are a type of Christ. In the Old Covenant, Moses gave stipulations about sacrificial lambs. The lamb had to be a male without defect; the offeror would lay hands on the lamb (symbolically transferring his sins to the animal) and then God would accept it as an atoning sacrifice (Lev 1:1-4). Likewise, Christ is called the "unblemished and spotless lamb" (1 Pet 1:19), in that he was perfect and without sin. He died to take away the sins of the world. John said this about Christ when he saw him approaching, "...Look, the Lamb of God, who takes away the sin of the world!" (John 1:29).

Christ's sacrifice is better than the blood of lambs because lambs could never take away sins—that is why they had to be

114

continually offered (Heb 10:1-4). However, Christ offered his body once and never again for the sins of the world. Sacrificial lambs were just a shadow of the one who would take away the sins of the world (Heb 10:11-14).

The Veil

The veil in the tabernacle and temple was a type of Christ. In the inner sanctuary of the tabernacle and temple (often called the Holy of Holies or the Most Holy Place), there was a veil which separated the Holy of Holies from the rest of the sanctuary. The Holy of Holies was where God's presence dwelled. Once a year on the Day of Atonement, the high priest would enter through the veil to offer sacrifices for sins. However, when Christ died on the cross, the veil in the temple was split—symbolizing how the hindrance into God's presence was removed. The writer of Hebrews says that now Christ's body is our veil (or "curtain")—his body is our doorway into the presence of God. Hebrews 10:19-20 says, "Therefore, brothers and sisters, since we have confidence to enter the sanctuary by the blood of Jesus, by the fresh and living way that he inaugurated for us through the curtain, that is, through his flesh."

Mercy Seat

Another type of Christ in the Old Testament is the "mercy seat," which was located in the Holy of Holies, within the tabernacle and temple. Romans 3:25 says this about Christ,

> God publicly displayed him [Jesus] at his death as the mercy seat accessible through faith. This was to demonstrate his righteousness, because God in his forbearance had passed over the sins previously committed.

In the Holy of Holies, there was a gold lid on the Ark of the Covenant. When the high priest entered, he placed drops of blood from a sacrificed lamb on the mercy seat. God would see this blood and spare the high priest, allowing him to have access to God. Jesus is our mercy seat. Because God sees his blood, which was shed for our sins, we have access to God at all times.

The Sabbath Day

The Old Testament Sabbath day is also a type of Christ. On the Sabbath day (Friday evening to Saturday evening), Jews were called to rest from their labor and worship God. In Colossians 2:16-17, Paul said this:

> Therefore do not let anyone judge you with respect to food or drink, or in the matter of a feast, new moon, or Sabbath days—these are only the shadow of the things to come, but the reality is Christ!

There were apparently false teachers in Colossae saying that believers still needed to practice the Old Testament Sabbath day. However, Paul argues that the Sabbath was a shadow of Christ, and now that Christ has come, believers no longer need to practice the Sabbath. Certainly, we still should practice the principle of Sabbath—resting from labor at least one day a week. Sabbath reminds us that we are not God—we need rest. Also, it reminds us that work is not our God, so we should not be enslaved to it. In Mark 2:27, Christ said, "The Sabbath was made for people, not people for the Sabbath." In Christ, we find our spiritual rest, which the Sabbath day always pointed to. In Matthew 11:28-30, Christ said,

Come to me, all you who are weary and burdened, and I will give you rest. Take my yoke on you and learn from me, because I am gentle and humble in heart, and you will find rest for your souls. For my yoke is easy to bear, and my load is not hard to carry.

Cities of Refuge

The Old Testament cities of refuge were a type of Christ. In the Mosaic Law, the Lord set aside six cities of refuge for people to run to when they had committed murder, whether on accident or on purpose. Since God had initiated the law of capital punishment for murder (Gen 9:6), he allowed those who were accused of murder to flee to the cities of refuge to escape the avenger of blood (usually a family member) and to have a fair trial. The verses below describe this:

> Now from these towns that you will give to the Levites you must select six towns of refuge to which a person who has killed someone may flee. And you must give them forty-two other towns.
> Numbers 35:6

> And they must stand as your towns of refuge from the avenger in order that the killer may not die until he has stood trial before the community.
> Numbers 35:12

The writer of Hebrews indicates that Christ is a type of "city of refuge." Hebrews 6:18-20 (ESV) says:

> so that by two unchangeable things, in which it is impossible for God to lie, we who have fled for refuge might

have strong encouragement to hold fast to the hope set before us. We have this as a sure and steadfast anchor of the soul, a hope that enters into the inner place behind the curtain, where Jesus has gone as a forerunner on our behalf, having become a high priest forever after the order of Melchizedek.

Previously, in Hebrews 6:8, the writer talked about being in danger of being cursed and destroyed by God for apostasy (turning away from God), then he describes the confidence of true believers who have "fled for refuge" to Jesus who is our "forerunner" and "high priest" (6:20). Since the wages of sin is death (Rom 6:23), we deserve death for sinning against God. However, those who run to the City of Refuge, Christ, shall be saved.

The Rock

In 1 Corinthians 10:1-4, Paul said this to the Corinthians:

For I do not want you to be unaware, brothers and sisters, that our fathers were all under the cloud and all passed through the sea, and all were baptized into Moses in the cloud and in the sea, and all ate the same spiritual food, and all drank the same spiritual drink. For they were all drinking from the spiritual rock that followed them, and the rock was Christ.

When Paul described a spiritual rock providing spiritual drink for Israel in the wilderness (v. 4), this story was very familiar to Jews since Moses provided water for Israel from a rock that he struck two different times—once near the beginning of their journey and again near the end (Ex 17:1-7, Num 20:2-13). Though Israel received water from a physical rock, Paul was saying that Christ ultimately supplied the water and that the rock Moses struck pictured the water's origin—Christ.[59] In fact, Jewish legend said that the initial rock that Moses struck followed Israel throughout their journey, supplying water for them.[60] John MacArthur's comments on this are helpful:

> I believe the apostle may have been alluding to this legend, saying, "Yes, a rock did follow Israel in the wilderness. But it was not a physical rock that provided merely physical water. It was a spiritual rock, the Messiah (the Hebrew term for Christ) whom you have long awaited, who was with our fathers even then."[61]

The rock in the wilderness which supplied water for Israel was a type of Christ—helping prepare Israel for their coming messiah.

David

David is a type of Christ. Scripture teaches that Christ is the prophesied Son of David who will one day rule on his father's throne over Israel and the world. However, sometimes in Scripture, Jesus is simply called David. For example, Ezekiel 37:24 says, "My servant David will be king over them; there will be one shepherd for all of them. They will follow my regulations and carefully observe my statutes." Because of this language, some people actually believe God will resurrect David to rule over Israel in the millennial kingdom (Rev 20). However, it seems that God is just using the name David to refer to the messiah, the Son of David. Jeremiah 23:5-6 says this:

> I, the LORD, promise that a new time will certainly come when I will raise up for them a righteous branch, a

descendant of David. He will rule over them with wisdom and understanding and will do what is just and right in the land. Under his rule Judah will enjoy safety and Israel will live in security. This is the name he will go by: 'The LORD has provided us with justice.'

Solomon

Solomon also is a type of Christ. In 1 Chronicles 17:11-14 (ESV), God made a covenant with David that he would have a son who would build God a house and have an everlasting rule. It says:

When your days are fulfilled to walk with your fathers, I will raise up your offspring after you, one of your own sons, and I will establish his kingdom. He shall build a house for me, and I will establish his throne forever. I will be to him a father, and he shall be to me a son. I will not take my steadfast love from him, as I took it from him who was before you, but I will confirm him in my house and in my kingdom forever, and his throne shall be established forever.

Solomon, David's son, did build the temple for God to dwell in. However, Solomon died, just like his father, David, did. Solomon only partially fulfilled God's promise. It is ultimately fulfilled in Christ—a future son of David. Christ also built God a house. Many have seen this fulfilled in at least two ways. (1) Christ built God a house by building the universal church, which is called the temple of God. In 1 Corinthians 3:16, Paul says this to the church, "Do you not know that you are God's temple and that God's Spirit lives in you?" Also, in 1 Peter 2:5, Peter says this to believers, "you yourselves, as living stones, are built up as a spiritual house to be a holy priesthood and to offer spiritual sacrifices that are acceptable to God through Jesus Christ." (2) But many also believe that Christ will one day build a future physical temple, even as Solomon did in his day. In Ezekiel 40-43, Ezekiel prophesies about the dimensions of a magnificent temple that has never yet been built, which many believe will exist during Christ's millennial reign on the earth (Rev 20).

Jonah

Jonah also was a type of Christ. When Jonah was in the big fish for three days and nights and then spit up onto dry land, that was a picture of Christ being in the earth for three days and nights and then resurrecting. In Matthew 12:38-41, Christ said this:

> Then some of the experts in the law along with some Pharisees answered him, "Teacher, we want to see a sign from you." But he answered them, "An evil and adulterous generation asks for a sign, but no sign will be given to it except the sign of the prophet Jonah. For just as Jonah was in the belly of the huge fish for three days and three nights, so the Son of Man will be in the heart of the earth for three days and three nights. The people of Nineveh will stand up at the judgment with this generation and condemn it, because they repented when Jonah preached to them—and now, something greater than Jonah is here!

Israel

The final typology of Christ we will consider is the nation of Israel. Matthew 2:14-15 pictures Israel as a type of Christ. It says:

> Then he got up, took the child and his mother during the night, and went to Egypt. He stayed there until Herod died.

In this way what was spoken by the Lord through the prophet was fulfilled: "I called my Son out of Egypt."

Matthew describes how Joseph and his family (including Jesus) hid in Egypt while Herod was executing babies in Israel. Then, Matthew quotes Hosea 11:1 which says, "I called my Son out of Egypt." Without close examination, it seems that Matthew was saying Christ fulfilled an Old Testament prophecy about him. However, Matthew is really describing how Israel was always a typology—a shadow which pictured the coming messiah. Hosea 11:1 says this: "When Israel was a young man, I loved him like a son, and I summoned my son out of Egypt." The quoted text, as originally written, had nothing to do with Christ. It originally was spoken by Hosea about how God called Israel out of Egypt, but Matthew uses it for how Joseph left Egypt with his son, Jesus, after initially fleeing there from Herod. This wasn't a prophecy; it was a typology. Matthew was saying Israel leaving Egypt was an Old Testament shadow of Christ. No doubt, Israel's forty years of being tempted and tried in the wilderness before going into the promised land was also meant to picture how Jesus was tempted and tried by the devil in the wilderness for forty days before beginning his ministry. However, where Israel failed God when tempted, Christ succeeded.

In fact, with the Servant Songs in Isaiah (Isaiah 42:1-4, 49:1-6, 50:4-9, 53), many struggle to discern when God is speaking about Israel or Jesus as the suffering servant. Sometimes it is clearly talking about Israel. At other times, it is clearly talking about Jesus (as in Isaiah 53), and sometimes, it is unclear. Consider Isaiah 49:1-6:

> Listen to me, you coastlands! Pay attention, you people who live far away! The LORD summoned me from birth; he commissioned me when my mother brought me into the

world. He made my mouth like a sharp sword, he hid me in the hollow of his hand; he made me like a sharpened arrow, he hid me in his quiver. He said to me, "You are my servant, Israel, through whom I will reveal my splendor." But I thought, "I have worked in vain; I have expended my energy for absolutely nothing." But the LORD will vindicate me; my God will reward me. So now the LORD says, the one who formed me from birth to be his servant—he did this to restore Jacob to himself, so that Israel might be gathered to him; and I will be honored in the LORD's sight, for my God is my source of strength—he says, "Is it too insignificant a task for you to be my servant, to reestablish the tribes of Jacob, and restore the remnant of Israel? I will make you a light to the nations, so you can bring my deliverance to the remote regions of the earth."

In verse 3, God calls the servant "Israel." But in verse 5, the servant is separate from Israel and is called to bring "Jacob" back to God. How do we explain this? Israel was meant to be a type of Christ—to reflect the future glory of the Savior to the Gentile world. However, because they failed God, the Savior, Jesus Christ, needed to turn the nation back to God and ultimately bring salvation to the unbelieving, Gentile world (v. 6). Israel is a type of Christ—a shadow of the greater reality.

Conclusion

In the Old Testament, there are many shadows of Christ—dim pictures of the greater reality. (1) This reminds us that God is the God of history, as it tells "His Story." He controls events in such a way that they testify of him and bring glory to him. God used stories such as the murder of Abel, Jacob's dream of a ladder, Moses delivering Israel from slavery in Egypt, Israel being bitten by snakes in the wilderness, Jonah being swallowed by a big fish, and much more, all to picture Christ and point people to salvation in Christ. (2) This not only reminds us that God is the author and controller of history, but also that the major theme of Scripture is Christ—not only the Old Testament but also the New Testament. The Old Testament prophesies about him and pictures him through types. The Gospels tell the story of his birth, life, death, and resurrection. The book of Acts shows the spread of Christ's gospel through his apostles. The Epistles declare his teaching through the apostles, and finally, Revelation describes Christ's wrath and coming to rule on the earth. Christ is the major theme of Scripture, and therefore, we must recognize him throughout and allow the pictures and messages about him to draw us to worship and obedience.

Reflection

1. Which types of Christ stood out most and why?
2. What types were new to you?
3. Should historical people like Isaac and Joseph be considered types of Christ when Scripture never clearly teaches that they are?
4. What other questions or applications did you take from the reading?

Study Group Tips

Leading a small group using the Bible Teacher's Guide can be done in various ways. One format for leading a small group is the "study group" model, where each member prepares and shares in the teaching. This appendix will cover tips for facilitating a weekly study group.

1. Each week the members of the study group will read through a selected chapter of the guide, answer the reflection questions (see Appendix 2), and come prepared to share with the group.

2. Prior to each meeting, a different member can be chosen to lead the group and share Question 1 of the reflection questions, which is to give a short summary of the chapter read. This section of the gathering could last from five to fifteen minutes. This way, each member can develop their gift of teaching. It also will make them study harder during the week. Or, each week the same person could share the summary.

3. After the summary has been given, the leader for that week will facilitate discussions through the rest of the reflection questions and also ask select review questions from the chapter.

4. After discussion, the group will share prayer requests and pray for one another.

The strength of the study group is the fact that the members will be required to prepare their responses before the meeting, which will allow for easier discussion. In addition, each member will be given the opportunity to teach, which will further equip their ministry skills. The study group model has distinct advantages.

Reflection Questions

Writing is one of the best ways to learn. In class, we take notes and write papers, and these methods are used to help us learn and retain the material. The same is true with the Word of God. Obviously, all the authors of Scripture were writers. This helped them better learn the Scriptures and also enabled them to more effectively teach it. As you reflect on God's Word, using the Bible Teacher's Guide, take time to write so you can similarly grow both in your learning and teaching.

1. How would you summarize the main points of the text/chapter? Write a brief summary.

2. What stood out to you most in the reading? Did any of the contents trigger any memories or experiences? If so, please share them.

3. What follow–up questions did you have about the reading? What parts did you not fully agree with?

4. What applications did you take from the reading, and how do you plan to implement them into your life?

5. Write several commitment statements: As a result of my time studying God's Word, I will . . .

6. What are some practical ways to pray as a result of studying the text? Spend some time ministering to the Lord through prayer.

Walking the Romans Road

How can a person be saved? From what is he saved? How can someone have eternal life? Scripture teaches that, after death, each person will spend eternity either in heaven or hell. How can a person go to heaven?

Paul said this to Timothy:

> You, however, must continue in the things you have learned and are confident about. You know who taught you and how from infancy you have known the holy writings, which are able to give you wisdom for salvation through faith in Christ Jesus.
> 2 Timothy 3:14-15

One of the reasons God gave us Scripture is to make us wise for salvation. This means that without it, nobody can know how to be saved.

Well then, how can a people be saved and what are they being saved from? A common method of sharing the good news of salvation is through the Romans Road. One of the great themes, not only of the Bible, but specifically of the book of Romans, is salvation. In Romans, the author, Paul, clearly details the steps we must take in order to be saved.

How can we be saved? What steps must we take?

Step One: We Must Accept that We Are Sinners

Romans 3:23 says, "For all have sinned and fall short of the glory of God." What does it mean to sin? The word sin means "to miss the mark." The mark we missed is reflecting God's image. When God created mankind in the Genesis narrative, he created man in the "image of God" (1:27). The "image of God" means many things, but most importantly it means we were made to be holy just as he is holy. Man was made moral. We were meant to reflect God's holiness in every way: the way we think, the way we talk, and the way we act. And any time we miss the mark in these areas, we commit sin.

Furthermore, we do not only sin when we commit a sinful act, such as lying, stealing, or cheating. We sin anytime we have a wrong heart motive. The greatest commandments in Scripture are to "Love the Lord your God with all your heart and to love your neighbor as yourself" (Matt 22:36-40, paraphrase). Whenever we don't love God supremely and love others as ourselves, we sin and fall short of the glory of God. For this reason, man is always in a state of sinning. Sadly, even if our actions are good, our heart is bad. I have never loved God with my whole heart, mind, and soul, and neither has anybody else. Therefore, we have all sinned and fall short of the glory of God (Rom 3:23). We have all missed the mark of God's holiness and we must accept this.

What's the next step?

Step Two: We Must Understand We Are Under the Judgment of God

Why are we under the judgment of God? It is because of our sins. Scripture teaches that God is not only a loving God, but he is also a just God. And his justice requires judgment for each of our sins. Romans 6:23 says, "For the payoff of sin is death."

A payoff or wage is something we earn. Every time we sin, we earn the wage of death. What is death? Death really means separation. In physical death, the body is separated from the spirit, but in spiritual death, man is separated from God. Man currently lives in a state of spiritual death (cf. Eph 2:1-3). We do not love God, obey him, or know him as we should. Therefore, man is in a state of death.

Moreover, on the day of our physical death, if we have not been saved, we will spend eternity separated from God in a very real hell. In hell, we will pay the wage for each of our sins. Therefore, in hell people will experience various degrees of punishment (cf. Lk 12:47-48). This places man in a very dangerous predicament—unholy and therefore under the judgment of God.

How should we respond to this? This leads us to our third step.

Step Three: We Must Recognize God Has Invited All to Accept His Free Gift of Salvation

Romans 6:23 does not stop at the wages of sin being death. It says, "For the payoff of sin is death, but the gift of God is eternal life in Christ Jesus our Lord." Because God loved everybody on the earth, he offered the free gift of eternal life, which anyone can receive through Jesus Christ.

Because it is a gift, it cannot be earned. We cannot work for it. Ephesians 2:8-9 says, "For by grace you are saved through faith, and this is not from yourselves, it is the gift of God; it is not from works, so that no one can boast."

Going to church, being baptized, giving to the poor, or doing any other righteous work does not save. Salvation is a gift that must be received from God. It is a gift that has been prepared by his effort alone.

How do we receive this free gift?

132

Step Four: We Must Believe Jesus Christ Died for Our Sins and Rose from the Dead

If we are going to receive this free gift, we must believe in God's Son, Jesus Christ. Because God loved us, cared for us, and didn't want us to be separated from him eternally, he sent his Son to die for our sins. Romans 5:8 says, "But God demonstrates his own love for us, in that while we were still sinners, Christ died for us." Similarly, John 3:16 says, "For this is the way God loved the world: He gave his one and only Son, so that everyone who believes in him will not perish but have eternal life." God so loved us that he gave his only Son for our sins.

Jesus Christ was a real, historical person who lived 2,000 years ago. He was born of a virgin. He lived a perfect life. He was put to death by the Romans and the Jews. And after he was buried, he rose again on the third day. In his death, he took our sins and God's wrath for those sins and gave us his perfect righteousness so we could be accepted by God. Second Corinthians 5:21 says, "God made the one who did not know sin to be sin for us, so that in him we would become the righteousness of God." God did all this so we could be saved from his wrath.

Christ's death satisfied the just anger of God over our sins. When God looked at Jesus on the cross, he saw us and our sins and therefore judged Jesus. And now, when God sees those of us who are saved, he sees his righteous Son and accepts us. In salvation, we have become the righteousness of God.

If we are going to be saved, if we are going to receive this free gift of salvation, we must believe in Christ's death, burial, and resurrection for our sins (cf. 1 Cor 15:3-5, Rom 10:9-10). Do you believe?

133

Step Five: We Must Confess Christ as Lord of Our Lives

Romans 10:9-10 says,

> Because if you confess with your mouth that Jesus is Lord and believe in your heart that God raised him from the dead, you will be saved. For with the heart one believes and thus has righteousness and with the mouth one confesses and thus has salvation.

Not only must we believe, but we must confess Christ as Lord of our lives. It is one thing to believe in Christ but another to follow Christ. Simple belief does not save. Christ must be our Lord. James said this: "...Even the demons believe that – and tremble with fear" (James 2:19), but the demons are not saved—Christ is not their Lord.

Another aspect of making Christ Lord is repentance. Repentance really means a change of mind that leads to a change of direction. Before we met Christ, we were living our own life and following our own sinful desires. But when we get saved, our mind and direction change. We start to follow Christ as Lord.

How do we make this commitment to the lordship of Christ so we can be saved? Paul said we must confess with our mouth "Jesus is Lord" as we believe in him. Romans 10:13 says, "For everyone who calls on the name of the Lord will be saved."

If you admit that you are a sinner and understand you are under God's wrath because of it; if you believe Jesus Christ is the Son of God, that he died on the cross for your sins, and rose from the dead for your salvation; if you are ready to turn from your sin and cling to Christ as Lord, you can be saved.

If this is your heart, then you can pray this prayer and commit to following Christ as your Lord.

Dear heavenly Father, I confess I am a sinner and have fallen short of your glory, what you made me for. I believe Jesus Christ died on the cross to pay the penalty for my sins and rose from the dead so I can have eternal life. I am turning away from my sin and accepting you as my Lord and Savior. Come into my life and change me. Thank you for your gift of salvation.

Scripture teaches that if you truly accept Christ as your Lord, then you are a new creation. Second Corinthians 5:17 says, "So then, if anyone is in Christ, he is a new creation; what is old has passed away – look, what is new has come!" God has forgiven your sins (1 John 1:9), he has given you his Holy Spirit (Rom 8:15), and he is going to disciple you and make you into the image of his Son (cf. Rom 8:29). He will never leave you nor forsake you (Heb 13:5), and he will complete the work he has begun in your life (Phil 1:6). In heaven, angels and saints are rejoicing because of your commitment to Christ (Lk 15:7).

Praise God for his great salvation! May God keep you in his hand, empower you through the Holy Spirit, train you through mature believers, and use you to build his kingdom! "He who calls you is trustworthy, and he will in fact do this" (1 Thess 5:24). God bless you!

Coming Soon

Praise the Lord for your interest in studying and teaching God's Word. If God has blessed you through the BTG series, please partner with us in petitioning God to greatly use this series to encourage and build his Church. Also, please consider leaving an Amazon review and signing up for free book promotions. By doing this, you help spread the "Word." Thanks for your partnership in the gospel from the first day until now (Phil 1:4-5).

Available:
First Peter
Theology Proper
Building Foundations for a Godly Marriage
Colossians
God's Battle Plan for Purity
Nehemiah
Philippians
The Perfections of God
The Armor of God
Ephesians
Abraham
Finding a Godly Mate
1 Timothy
The Beatitudes
Equipping Small Group Leaders
2 Timothy

About the Author

Greg Brown earned his MA in religion and MA in teaching from Trinity International University, a MRE from Liberty University, and a PhD in theology from Louisiana Baptist University. He has served over sixteen years in pastoral ministry and currently serves as a chaplain and professor at Handong Global University, teaching pastor at Handong International Congregation, and as a Navy Reserve chaplain.

Greg married his lovely wife, Tara Jayne, in 2006, and they have one daughter, Saiyah Grace. He enjoys going on dates with his wife, playing with his daughter, reading, writing, studying in coffee shops, working out, and following the NBA and UFC. His pursuit in life, simply stated, is "to know God and to be found faithful by Him."

To connect with Greg, please follow at http://www.pgregbrown.com.

Notes

1 Grudem, W. A. (2004). <u>Systematic theology: an introduction to biblical doctrine</u> (p. 544). Leicester, England; Grand Rapids, MI: Inter-Varsity Press; Zondervan Pub. House.

2 Grudem, W. A. (2004). <u>Systematic theology: an introduction to biblical doctrine</u> (p. 544). Leicester, England; Grand Rapids, MI: Inter-Varsity Press; Zondervan Pub. House.

3 Aaron, Daryl. Understanding Theology in 15 Minutes a Day: How can I know God?

4 Aaron, Daryl. Understanding Theology in 15 Minutes a Day: How can I know God? Baker Publishing Group. Kindle Edition.

5 Aaron, Daryl. Understanding Theology in 15 Minutes a Day: How can I know God? Baker Publishing Group. Kindle Edition.

6 Evans, Tony. Theology You Can Count On: Experiencing What the Bible Says About... God the Father, God the Son, God the Holy Spirit, Angels, Salvation... Moody Publishers. Kindle Edition.

7 Evans, Tony. Theology You Can Count On: Experiencing What the Bible Says About... God the Father, God the Son, God the Holy Spirit, Angels, Salvation... Moody Publishers. Kindle Edition.

8 Accessed 8/4/20 from https://www.thegospelcoalition.org/article/you-asked-did-jesus-assume-a-fallen-human-nature/

9 Accessed 8/4/20 from https://www.thegospelcoalition.org/article/you-asked-did-jesus-assume-a-fallen-human-nature/

10 Accessed 4/8/20 from https://carm.org/jesus-chist/what-does-it-mean-that-jesus-was-made-in-the-likeness-of-sinful-flesh

11 Consider the arguments against the Fallen Human Nature view in these articles: accessed 8/4/20 from https://www.thegospelcoalition.org/article/you-asked-did-jesus-assume-a-fallen-human-nature/ and https://carm.org/jesus-chist/what-does-it-mean-that-jesus-was-made-in-the-likeness-of-sinful-flesh

[12] MacArthur, J. F., Jr. (1983). Hebrews (p. 112). Chicago: Moody Press.

[13] Grudem, W. A. (2004). Systematic theology: an introduction to biblical doctrine (p. 568). Leicester, England; Grand Rapids, MI: Inter-Varsity Press; Zondervan Pub. House.

[14] Accessed 7/22/20 from https://www.gotquestions.org/Old-Testament-believers.html

[15] Accessed 7/22/20 from https://www.gotquestions.org/Old-Testament-believers.html

[16] MacArthur, J. F., Jr. (1986). Ephesians (p. 138). Chicago: Moody Press.

[17] MacArthur, J. F., Jr. (1986). Ephesians (p. 140). Chicago: Moody Press.

[18] Grudem, W. A. (2004). Systematic theology: an introduction to biblical doctrine (p. 608). Leicester, England; Grand Rapids, MI: Inter-Varsity Press; Zondervan Pub. House.

[19] Evans, Tony. Theology You Can Count On: Experiencing What the Bible Says About... God the Father, God the Son, God the Holy Spirit, Angels, Salvation... Moody Publishers. Kindle Edition.

[20] Grudem, W. A. (2004). Systematic theology: an introduction to biblical doctrine (p. 615). Leicester, England; Grand Rapids, MI: Inter-Varsity Press; Zondervan Pub. House.

[21] Evans, Tony. Theology You Can Count On: Experiencing What the Bible Says About... God the Father, God the Son, God the Holy Spirit, Angels, Salvation... . Moody Publishers. Kindle Edition.

[22] Grudem, W. A. (2004). Systematic theology: an introduction to biblical doctrine (p. 615). Leicester, England; Grand Rapids, MI: Inter-Varsity Press; Zondervan Pub. House.

[23] Ryrie, C. C. (1999). Basic Theology: A Popular Systematic Guide to Understanding Biblical Truth (p. 310). Chicago, IL: Moody Press.

[24] Grudem, W. A. (2004). Systematic theology: an introduction to biblical doctrine (p. 619). Leicester, England; Grand Rapids, MI: Inter-Varsity Press; Zondervan Pub. House.

[25] Accessed 1/13/2020 from http://content.time.com/time/specials/packages/article/0,28804,2111975_2112269_2112278,00.html

[26] Accessed 7/22/20 from https://billygraham.org/devotion/evidence-of-jesus/

[27] Bright, Bill. A Journey Home. Thomas Nelson Publishers. 2003.

[28] McDowell, Josh. Evidence That Demands a Verdict (p. 276). Thomas Nelson. Kindle Edition.

[29] McDowell, Josh. Evidence That Demands a Verdict (p. 276-277). Thomas Nelson. Kindle Edition.

[30] McDowell, Josh. Evidence That Demands a Verdict (p. 268). Thomas Nelson. Kindle Edition.

[31] Accessed 7/24/2020 from https://www.gotquestions.org/why-believe-resurrection.html

[32] Accessed 7/24/2020 from https://www.gotquestions.org/why-believe-resurrection.html

[33] McDowell, Josh. Evidence That Demands a Verdict (p. 262). Thomas Nelson. Kindle Edition.

[34] McDowell, Josh. Evidence That Demands a Verdict (p. 262). Thomas Nelson. Kindle Edition.

[35] Accessed 1/13/2020 from https://www.josh.org/wp-content/uploads/Easter-Articles-Who-Would-die-for-a-lie.pdf

[36] Accessed 1/13/2019 from https://seanmcdowell.org/blog/did-james-the-brother-of-jesus-die-as-a-martyr

[37] McDowell, Joshua. More Than a Carpenter. Chapter "Did You Hear What Happened to Saul?"

[38] McDowell, Joshua. More Than a Carpenter. Chapter "Did You Hear What Happened to Saul?"

[39] Bright, Bill. A Journey Home. Thomas Nelson Publishers. 2003.

[40] Hitchcock, Mark. The Amazing Claims of Bible Prophecy, (p. 86). Harvest House Publishers. Kindle Edition.

[41] Accessed 7/27/20 from https://enduringword.com/bible-commentary/mark-6/

[42] Accessed 7/27/20 from https://enduringword.com/bible-commentary/john-8/

[43] MacArthur, J. F., Jr. (1985). Matthew (Vol. 1, p. 3). Chicago: Moody Press.

[44] MacDonald, W. (1995). Believer's Bible Commentary: Old and New Testaments. (A. Farstad, Ed.) (p. 1379). Nashville: Thomas Nelson.

[45] Accessed 7/27/2020 from https://www.christianity.com/wiki/bible/what-is-the-meaning-of-hosanna-in-the-bible.html

[46] Accessed 7/27/2020 from https://www.christiancourier.com/articles/1556-importance-of-messianic-genealogy-the

[47] Rydelnik, M. A. (2014). Daniel. In The moody bible commentary (p. 1305). Chicago, IL: Moody Publishers.

[48] Hitchcock, Mark. The Amazing Claims of Bible Prophecy, (p. 46). Harvest House Publishers. Kindle Edition.

[49] Rydelnik, M. A. (2014). Daniel. In The moody bible commentary (p. 1306). Chicago, IL: Moody Publishers.

[50] Rydelnik, M. A. (2014). Daniel. In The moody bible commentary (p. 1306). Chicago, IL: Moody Publishers.

[51] "Micah" accessed 8/6/19 from https://www.biblica.com/resources/scholar-notes/niv-study-bible/intro-to-micah/ 142

[52] McDowell, Josh. Evidence That Demands a Verdict (p. 231). Thomas Nelson. Kindle Edition.

[53] Accessed 7/27/20 from https://www.foxnews.com/politics/christian-persecution-how-many-are-being-killed-where-they-are-being-killed

[54] Accessed 4/9/20 from https://www.nytimes.com/2020/03/10/world/asia/south-korea-coronavirus-shincheonji.html

[55] Accessed 7/21/20 from http://www.earlychristianwritings.com/talmud.html

[56] McDowell, Josh. Evidence That Demands a Verdict (p. 346). Thomas Nelson. Kindle Edition.

[57] Evans, Tony. Theology You Can Count On: Experiencing What the Bible Says About... God the Father, God the Son, God the Holy Spirit, Angels, Salvation... Moody Publishers. Kindle Edition.

[58] Hart, J. F. (2014). John. In M. A. Rydelnik & M. Vanlaningham (Eds.), The moody bible commentary (p. 1608). Chicago, IL: Moody Publishers.

[59] Vanlaningham, M. G. (2014). 1 Corinthians. In M. A. Rydelnik & M. Vanlaningham (Eds.), The moody bible commentary (pp. 1788–1789). Chicago, IL: Moody Publishers.

[60] MacArthur, J. F., Jr. (1984). 1 Corinthians (p. 220). Chicago: Moody Press.

[61] MacArthur, J. F., Jr. (1984). 1 Corinthians (p. 220). Chicago: Moody Press.